Praise for the series:

It was only a matter of time before a clever publisher realized that there is an audience for whom *Exile on Main Street* or *Electric Ladyland* are as significant and worthy of study as *The Catcher in the Rye* or *Middlemarch* . . . The series . . . is freewheeling and eclectic, ranging from minute rock-geek analysis to idiosyncratic personal celebration—*The New York Times Book Review*

Ideal for the rock geek who thinks liner notes just aren't enough—*Rolling Stone*

One of the coolest publishing imprints on the planet—*Bookslut*

These are for the insane collectors out there who appreciate fantastic design, well-executed thinking, and things that make your house look cool. Each volume in this series takes a seminal album and breaks it down in startling minutiae. We love these. We are huge nerds—*Vice*

A brilliant series . . . each one a work of real love—*NME* (UK)

Passionate, obsessive, and smart—*Nylon*

Religious tracts for the rock 'n' roll faithful—*Boldtype*

[A] consistently excellent series—*Uncut* (UK)

We . . . aren't naive enough to think that we're your only source for reading about music (but if we had our way . . . watch out). For those of you who really like to know everything there is to know about an album, you'd do well to check out Bloomsbury's "33 1/3" series of books—*Pitchfork*

For almost 20 years, the 33-and-a-Third series of music books has focused on individual albums by acts well known (Bob Dylan, Nirvana, Abba, Radiohead), cultish (Neutral Milk Hotel, Throbbing Gristle, Wire) and many levels in-between. The range of music and their creators defines "eclectic," while the writing veers from freewheeling to acutely insightful. In essence, the books are for the music fan who (as Rolling Stone noted) "thinks liner notes just aren't enough."—*The Irish Times*

For reviews of individual titles in the series, please visit our blog at 333sound.com and our website at https://www.bloomsbury.com/academic/music-sound-studies/

Follow us on Twitter: @333books

Like us on Facebook: https://www.facebook.com/33.3books

For a complete list of books in this series, see the back of this book.

Forthcoming in the series:

and many more . . .

Time's Up

Kimberly Mack

BLOOMSBURY ACADEMIC
NEW YORK • LONDON • OXFORD • NEW DELHI • SYDNEY

BLOOMSBURY ACADEMIC
Bloomsbury Publishing Inc
1385 Broadway, New York, NY 10018, USA
50 Bedford Square, London, WC1B 3DP, UK
29 Earlsfort Terrace, Dublin 2, Ireland

BLOOMSBURY, BLOOMSBURY ACADEMIC and the Diana logo are trade-
marks of Bloomsbury Publishing Plc

First published in the United States of America 2023

A catalog record for this book is available from the Library of Congress.

ISBN: PB: 978-1-5013-7751-8
ePDF: 978-1-5013-7753-2
eBook: 978-1-5013-7752-5

Series: 33 ⅓

Typeset by Deanta Global Publishing Services, Chennai, India
Printed and bound in Great Britain

To find out more about our authors and books visit www.bloomsbury.com
and sign up for our newsletters.

Contents

Figures

Introduction

I reached out, hoping to grab my friend Aleeka's hand, but I could only see legs. I made myself as small as I could, crouching down and wrapping my arms around my head in a defensive stance. I was at the bottom of the mosh pit, and I was beginning to feel sick from the heat and close bodies. When I was able to stand, I strained to see the stage where singer Corey Glover of the band Living Colour was losing his mind, singing as if his life depended on it, while bassist Muzz Skillings provided a loud and hypnotic heartbeat, Will Calhoun absolutely pummeled the drums, and guitarist Vernon Reid played a monster metal riff.

I was mesmerized. It was December 1990 and my first Living Colour show. We were at the Academy in midtown Manhattan, and the band was touring behind 1990's *Time's Up*. I was an amateur in the New York City hardcore scene, while Matt, who I had only been dating for five months, was a regular at weekend matinee hardcore shows at the famed music club CBGBs. Slam dancing was what he did every weekend to blow off a little steam, while I enjoyed shows that were, shall we say, a bit tamer.

Even though Living Colour wasn't really a hardcore band, they had hardcore and metal songs in their repertoire that were perfect to mosh to: loud, cacophonic, and aggressive songs that were the perfect soundtrack of slamming bodies. The band had barely started their first song "New Jack Theme" when a chasm formed in the middle of the crowd and a rapidly growing group of young men ran around the center in a frenzy. Before long I lost sight of Aleeka and Matt. As I did my best to stay out of the fray, I locked eyes with a Black guy wearing tiny dreads and a Black Flag T-shirt. He walked over to me, grabbed me firmly with both hands on my shoulders, and, smiling in a way that I can only describe as demonic, uttered "There you go!" and pushed me hard into the mosh pit. I stayed on my feet for less than a minute. Bodies were crashing into me with such force that I went down fast. Then I felt a hand gripping my arm. It was Matt. He pulled me up and led me out of the circle of violently colliding, sweaty bodies.

*　*　*

That night on the stage in front of the mosh pit at the Academy, Living Colour was supporting their new album *Time's Up* and coming off their hugely successful debut *Vivid*. Their 1988 release was eventually certified double platinum (two million copies) and reached number six on the US Billboard 200 chart. The single "Cult of Personality" made it to number thirteen on the Billboard Hot 100 chart and number nine on the Billboard Mainstream Rock Airplay chart. "Cult of Personality" ("Look in my eyes, what do you see? The cult of personality/I know your anger, I know your dreams. I've been everything you want to be. Oh I'm the cult of personality") won a Grammy for Best Hard Rock Performance. *Vivid* was also well reviewed, with publications like *Rolling Stone* and the *New York Times* showering the album and the band with praise.[1,2,3]

But Living Colour also had its detractors. Some critics and rock fans disapproved of four young Black men choosing to play rock music instead of hip-hop or R&B, while others were dismissive of the style in which they played rock music. In a review of *Vivid* for Brooklyn's *City Sun*, a Black weekly newspaper, Armond White famously excoriated Living Colour for following "the strictest–whitest–ideas of what rock music should be" and participating in "the imitation of white rock idioms."[4] And in a 2014 interview I did with Reid, he said, "I remember one time we were playing a show. It was a show at a college. I remember a girl, a Black girl. She was talking about us to someone, and she said, 'They sound like a copy of a copy of a copy.' It really stung." For some on both sides of the color line, rock music (particularly subgenres like metal or hardcore) is unassailably White music.

Given the segregated nature of the record industry during the 1980s, with artists tethered to strict, race-based musical categories, and the resistance Black rockers sometimes faced from both White rock audiences and skeptics in the Black community, Living Colour's success was entirely unexpected. Formed in 1984 by Reid (vocals and guitar) as a trio with bassist Alex Mosely and drummer Greg Carter, with several more lineup changes before settling on the *Vivid/Time's Up* quartet, Living Colour fielded challenges from all directions.

Reid would later cofound the Black Rock Coalition (BRC) with legendary music critic Greg Tate and producer Konda Mason, which advocated for Black musicians to have the opportunity to play, and make a living playing, music within the full constellation of Black expression, including rock. In a 2014 interview I did with Glover, he told the following story about an encounter with a Black ex-bandmate:

> The people I used to sing with I saw one day on the subway. I had left them some years earlier and they knew I was in this band. The guy said to me, "When are you gonna stop doing this nonsense, and do some real music?" Everyone thought that this was some sort of fluke, that I was doing this—that we were all doing this—as a way to get attention for what we really wanted to do, which was Black music.

And Reid describes people's reactions to Living Colour in the early days this way:

> There was complete and utter resistance. This is not going to happen. Forget about it. You're dreaming. Have a nice trip. Good luck with that. All of that. And this was the response from a lot of different people. Not just White people. And a lot of folks were in our corner, too. Don't get me wrong. And some of those folks kept me going.

Living Colour persevered, and when Mick Jagger of the Rolling Stones saw the band play at CBGBs one night and agreed to produce their demo, doors opened and the band finally landed their major label deal with Epic Records. While opening for the Stones during their 1989 North American *Steel Wheels* tour, *Vivid* raced up the charts.

As Living Colour's fame grew, the band faced new criticisms as the circumstances behind their success rankled some in the BRC. As Maureen Mahon in her book *Right to Rock: The Black Rock Coalition and the Cultural Politics of Race* states, "That Living Colour got its deal in part through the support of a white English rock star who symbolizes the white appropriation of Black culture was troubling to some members."[5] Not only were some folks in the BRC unhappy with Living Colour's success, resulting from what they saw as White patronage of the worst kind, but others were unhappy that Living Colour was the only band in the organization that enjoyed mainstream success. According to Reid:

> The hardest thing and really the ugliest, weirdest thing for me was: "So Vernon Reid sets up the Black Rock Coalition and then his band gets all the shine." I don't know what to do with that. It's so strange because The BRC was an outgrowth of just reaching out to friends that were part of a kind of unnamed community. We were all doing different shit. . . . The idea of it being some kind of grand design for my band to take advantage of is not true.

But perhaps most disturbingly, in the aftermath of their newfound success, despite the political nature of their lyrics and their willingness to engage publicly such hot-button topics as racism, the drug wars, police brutality, and other salient political and social concerns facing Black people in America, Living Colour soon braced themselves against the salvo of sellout.

Rock authenticity, particularly in the late 1980s/early 1990s, was a highly prized commodity. Theodore Gracyk in *Rhythm and Noise: An Aesthetics of Rock* states, "Given the premise that the true artist must genuinely *mean* whatever is said, and that anything else is commercial manipulation, the charge of sellout has been the most damning one that can be brought against a rock musician. . . . Anyone in rock who becomes widely popular is immediately prone to backlash."[6] Living Colour's celebrity, ironically, placed them on the outside looking into the Black rock clubhouse, even putting them in opposition to important Black rock bands like 24-7 SPYZ and Fishbone. "You read an article and people would take potshots once the band was successful. It was hurtful," Reid said. So not only did their mainstream success indicate to the hardcore/indie rock crowd that they must have compromised their artistic integrity in some way but they also were not seen as authentically Black enough to resonate with Black audiences. Mahon explains:

> Living Colour, a black band marketed chiefly to the white rock audience, was more vulnerable to suspicions about their authenticity than black artists who were initially marketed to black audiences before being "crossed over." . . . In a context with sharply demarcated visions of how black musicians should sound, it seemed fair to ask what it meant for a consciously black band like Living Colour to play for mostly white fans. Perhaps they were just "selling out."[7]

So, confusingly, the band were accused of selling out by different musician peers and audiences for competing reasons.

After succeeding beyond what anyone predicted and evolving away from the need to conform to the sonic expectations of critics and fans, or chasing commercial success, their next release in 1990 reflected significant creative growth. When Living Colour went in the studio to record their sophomore effort, *Time's Up*, the band hoped to use this record to say something new. "*Time's Up* is a very different record than *Vivid*," Reid said. "The perspective of it. There's a kind of optimistic dystopia. Dystopian optimism— that's the best way I would describe what was going on at that time." It is not surprising that the record would be edgier and more confrontational than *Vivid* and less easily categorized. Not only was Living Colour battling all the naysayers, but in the early 1990s, when the record was released, there was an abrupt shift in the type of music that was commercially successful (notably Nirvana knocking hair metal bands and pop artists off the charts). Even clothing and performance styles changed almost overnight. Not surprisingly, Living Colour's look changed from *Vivid* to *Time's Up* with button-down shirts replacing Day-Glo and jeans replacing spandex body gloves and racing pants. *Time's Up* begins with the title track "Time's Up," a blistering, hardcore environmental crisis wake-up call. In the middle of the record is "Elvis Is Dead," a funky, absurdist examination of delusional Elvis Presley fans, complete with a critique of his mythical status and cameos by Little Richard, Maceo Parker, and Mick Jagger, who gamely utters the words "Elvis is dead" during the breakdown. The disc ends with "This Is the Life," a psychedelic take on learning to accept the life you have.

Time's Up is an important record because after two years of being trapped in the political-activist-funk-metal box, Living Colour was able to break out with an innovative rock album that served as the sonic representation of their diverse backgrounds and interest in racial, political, and social justice. And the album *Time's Up* continues to be important in the 2020s. As activists take to the streets to protest White supremacy, anti-Black racism, and the continued devaluation of Black lives, *Time's Up* revisits, affirms, and amplifies Black participation in, and vital contributions to, rock music. Living Colour's sophomore effort holds great relevance in light of its forward-thinking politics and lyrical engagement with issues that remain critical and current.

When I first heard the apocalyptic alarm clock and the violent snap of Calhoun's drum at the beginning of "Time's Up," it felt like a hammer hitting me in the head. It was angry. It was violent. It was disturbing. And I fell in love with it immediately.

* * *

When I was nineteen, I thought rock was White, and my love of it rendered me an interloper. I believed this even as my mom and I watched Living Colour perform "Open Letter (to a Landlord)" from *Vivid* on *It's Showtime at the Apollo* in the spring of 1989 in our Brooklyn living room. Their song, "Cult of Personality," was everywhere, and Reid's ferocious opening riff played on a loop in my brain in the fall of 1988. I remember feeling annoyed that the band didn't play their hard rock hit and instead played what I perceived at the time as softer, poppier songs ("Open Letter" and "Broken Hearts") that showcased Glover's gospel-inflected vocal chops. In my mind, this was a capitulation to the largely Black Apollo crowd that likely also viewed rock as White but who, unlike me, preferred R&B or hip-hop, styles of music normatively viewed as Black.

But even though I wanted Living Colour to rock out, my desires felt transgressive. I had been a passionate fan of rock music since I was nine, but I still felt like the music didn't belong to me. After all, I grew up in the Marcy Housing Projects in Brooklyn. I wasn't the target demographic for MTV. This was certainly the message I received loud and clear in the late 1980s from the music industry, with its rigid, race-based genres; from rock radio; from MTV; and at the many live concerts I attended when I could usually count the number of Black people besides myself on one hand.

While Living Colour was always clear about rock music's Black origins and found solidarity within the Black Rock Coalition, they fought an uphill battle as they worked to overcome music industry resistance to the idea of an all-Black rock band. Yet they accomplished the seemingly impossible, breaking into the mainstream rock market.

In 1984, at fifteen, I saw the video for "Rock Box" by Run-DMC. I already knew a little something about hip-hop: I had memorized all the words to 1979's "Rapper's Delight" by the Sugarhill Gang, and I liked cuts by Kurtis Blow, Grandmaster Flash and the Furious Five, and Afrika Bambaataa. I sensed the same rebellion in these tracks that I appreciated in rock music. I had also gone with my younger cousin to neighborhood block parties where MCs rocked the mic and b-boys and b-girls danced frenetically during song breaks. I bore witness to the formation of a new musical style that was conceived and performed by Black people, but I had never heard a hip-hop song that melded rap and rock styles. In "Rock Box," Eddie Martinez's electric rock guitar was front and center in both the distinctive riff and the searing guitar breaks. I was transfixed by the shots of Martinez in the video, a man of color, in a serious rock stance playing distorted electric guitar. In that moment, for the first time, I thought it might not be taboo to be a Black person who loves rock music.

But this feeling was short-lived.

In this book, I look at a band who was trying to become itself in the face of a music industry and fans who weren't sure how to react to them. Focusing on their second album, *Time's Up*, I explore how they weathered these responses and made a history-making body of music in the process. Rather than remaining in the pop-funk-metal box in which critics had placed them, Living Colour created a timeless record that is the musical embodiment—confident, jarring, fierce, collaborative, and hybrid—of their diverse backgrounds and commitment to racial, political, and social justice. The clash of sounds and styles don't immediately fit. The confrontational hardcore-thrash metal complete with Glover's apocalyptic wail in the title track is not a natural companion with Doug E. Fresh's human beatbox on "Tag Team Partners," but it is precisely this bold and brilliant collision that creates the barely controlled chaos. And isn't rock and roll about chaos?

Through interviews with members of Living Colour and others involved in the making of *Time's Up*, I explore the creation and reception of this artistically challenging work, while examining the legacy of this culturally important and groundbreaking American rock band. *Time's Up* weaves together the story and impact of the band, an oral history of the making of *Time's Up*, and cultural criticism focused on the music and critical reception of the album and Living Colour's meaning and influence on both American music history and my musical education. The narrative is framed by my coming of age with rock music and with Living Colour, from mosh pit days to the work I do as a scholar and music critic.

After all, it was Living Colour who finally got through to me. In 1990, while visiting home during my senior year at New York University, my mother and I sat on the living room couch and watched, again, transfixed, while Living Colour performed "Pride" from *Time's Up* on *It's Showtime at the Apollo*. We didn't speak until the song was over. We were both mesmerized by these four young Black men who not only rocked hard but also saw the political importance of playing at the Apollo and winning over the predominantly Black audience on their own terms. Living Colour not only gave me permission to love rock music but also inspired me, through songs like "Pride" ("Don't ask me why I play this music./'Cause it's my culture so naturally I use it."), to learn more about the Black origins of rock and roll and rock music.

And I did.

I had the distinct honor of interviewing all four current members of Living Colour, as well as former bass player, Muzz Skillings, for this book. I also interviewed vital contributors to the production of *Time's Up* such as producer Ed Stasium; engineer Paul Hamingson; Greg Drew, Glover's vocal coach; Dennis Diamond, Reid's guitar tech; and the late music critic and journalist, cofounder of the Black Rock Coalition, and friend to Living Colour, Greg Tate. Tate's contributions to

American cultural criticism cannot be overstated. He was one of the earliest hip-hop critics, and he also wrote about rock and other forms of Black popular music and Black popular culture with an unparalleled poetic intellectualism. He has influenced, challenged, and mentored countless music writers, including myself, and his passion for making sense of Black art was always palpable and infectious. All quotations from the band members, their production team, and Greg Tate are from interviews conducted by me in 2014, 2021, and 2022, unless noted otherwise.

1
"History Lesson"
Who Are Living Colour?

The musicians in Living Colour came together in late 1980s New York City, among early rap and hardcore, nestled within a melting pot of immigrants who had arrived from all over the world. The paths they and their families took to get there were both panoramic and unique, which would match the band members' first meetings. Corey Glover and Vernon Reid met at a birthday party when Glover recalls that Reid came up to him and said, after Glover's "Happy Birthday" rendition: "That sounds really good. Do you do this professionally?" Glover was trying to start a band with some friends who attended school with him at Dowling College on Long Island. "None of us played any instruments whatsoever," Glover recalls.

It's the eighties and everyone plays a synthesizer with everybody, so you can get away with it, you know? And I knew three chords then, and I know three chords now. So in this conversation with Vernon, I'm thinking he'd be a great guitar player for my band, not knowing just how involved his history was, and how much of a musician he really was.

Guitarist Reid would find the inspiration to pursue music in earnest after meeting a group of serious musicians at Brooklyn Technical High School, including drummers Reggie Sylvester and Trevor Gale. Another such musician was Raymond Jones, a pianist and keyboardist who would join Chic at nineteen and later worked as a composer and producer for multiple Spike Lee films. "We met in the back of history class, and he was a committed musician," Reid said. "That influenced me to pick the guitar up again at sixteen and take lessons." Reid had grown up in a home where, as he put it, there were no "guardrails" around the music that his family listened to or the other culture they consumed. By seventeen, Reid's guitar playing had reached another level. "I played all guitar all the time to the annoyance and the anxiety of my parents." Like the rest of Living Colour, his musical interests were eclectic. "Things that move me and things that I connect to can be very avant-garde and very complex and very strange, but also simple, basic ass shit," he said. "You know, the 'Humpty Dance' basic, things that just make it move." The avant-garde musical dynamisms crossed with rock and that "basic shit" would influence the band's sound: the dreamy psychedelia of "This Is the Life" and the off-the-wall guitar soundscapes in "Information Overload" that can be found on *Time's Up*.

Drummer Will Calhoun's coming of age was one of wide musical influences and full of the history of the Great Migration of Black southerners coming North and of Black history more generally. He grew up in a "very Afrocentric, historical house." Calhoun said:

I didn't realize it at the time, but as I got older, when I did my book reports, we had statutes of Mary McLeod Bethune and George Washington Carver. . . . It was nice to go to school and do reports on things that none of my friends knew about, or even sometimes my teachers. But my parents are very much into us knowing a) about Africa and the culture there, but also b) about what was Black.

Bassist Muzz Skillings, who grew up in Southeast Queens, brought both a household appreciation of a range of music to the band and what he absorbed studying the origins and influences of music as an ethnomusicology student at the City College of New York (CCNY). "I learned the difference between a musical expression which can resemble a particular genre of music as opposed to a musical expression, which has all the core accepted and agreed upon ingredients, which define a genre of music," Skillings said.

The men in Living Colour came of age after the civil rights and Black power movements had ended. They were old enough to bear witness to the previous era's political strife, but by the time they emerged into adulthood during the 1980s they found a particularly vibrant middle-class Black artistic landscape. One that, due to increased Black and White social and cultural engagement, allowed for a new way of approaching Black art. This, of course, did not mean that racism was solved and Black art and (most importantly) Black people were seen, heard, and valued. As Trey Ellis puts it in his 1989 article, "The New Black Aesthetic" (for which a young Reid was quoted), "We realize that despite this current buppie artist boom, most black Americans have seldom had it worse."[1] Nevertheless, we can see the ways in which the New Black Aesthetic or post-soul[2] operate in the lives of the culturally omnivorous members of Living Colour.

But long before that article was published and decades before these men would meet, their families had to find their way to the boroughs of New York to begin new lives.

Reid's parents arrived in London during the 1950s from a small town called Gages in Montserrat, part of the Leeward Islands situated where the Caribbean intersects the Western Atlantic Ocean. As they traveled to London from what was then a British colony, and is still today a British territory, to help in the post–Second World War cleanup efforts, it is unlikely that they were prepared for the hostile reception they would face in the form of a Colour Bar (British-style Jim Crow). "It was common in the windows of rented flats to find: 'No colored. No Irish. No dogs.'"[3] This culminated in mass racial violence during the Notting Hill riots in the summer of 1958.

Reid was born to this young couple on August 22, 1958, in London, one day before the Notting Hill riots' opening salvo.[4] "We talk about the great migration from the South to the North [In the United States], and, you know, to the Midwest and the Northeast, and there was another almost parallel migration from the Caribbean, which was really post World War II," Reid said of his parents. "The people who came from Pakistan, people who came from Nigeria, people who came from Jamaica, and also Trinidad, and also smaller islands like Montserrat came for opportunity and to rebuild the nation, to rebuild the industrial cities that had been blitzkrieged."

It was the very real threat of racial violence that would lead to Reid's parents' decision to leave the UK. In the late 1950s, London's Notting Hill was an economically depressed neighborhood with rampant crime. But it offered Blacks housing, albeit usually overpriced and overcrowded. The West Indian immigrants lived in run-down tenements in Colville, while the White working class lived in Notting Dale. Racial tensions simmered, as some Whites saw the Black newcomers as competition for the few meager available resources.[5] What began as a racism of the most insidious and structural kind, over time evolved into a brutal hatred on the streets. "The so-called Teddy Boys, who were kind of rockabilly, their thing was they were patterning themselves after rockabilly [with] particular pompadour type hair styles, but they also were very anti-immigrant," Reid said. "And the rise of anti-immigrant sentiment started to really disturb [my parents]."

On Saturday, August 23, 1958, a mob of nine young White men roved the streets of Notting Hill, as they put it, "Nigger hunting," resulting in numerous injuries and hospitalizations of Black people. And one week later, on Saturday, August 30, the riot began in earnest, with yet more White men searching for Black people to injure, intimidate, or both. The riots lasted until Wednesday, September 3, and at first West Indian residents were terrified—afraid to leave their houses to buy groceries. Afraid to walk the streets on the way home after work. The police were no help, as they would arrest the Black people who fought back. But fight back they did, and with the help of Jamaicans from Brixton, the rampage came to an end.[6,7]

Reid's parents "decided to take a chance on America." They first lived in Harlem, but they soon moved to Brooklyn, to the border of Bed-Stuy and Crown Heights, where they had extended family. "The Caribbean is not a monolith," Reid said. His father was a mail sorter at the US Postal Service and an early computer programmer, who eventually became an air traffic controller. His mother worked for 1199 Health & Hospital Workers Union in membership services. Reid lived with his parents and two younger sisters, who were born in the United States in 1963 and 1968. When Reid's family purchased a home on Empire Boulevard, they "became the first Black family on the block."

Calhoun's mother and father were part of that other Great Migration. The one where scores of Black Southern Americans moved to the Northeast, the Midwest, and the West during the first half of the twentieth century in search of better jobs and economic circumstances. Calhoun was born in Brooklyn Hospital on July 22, 1964—"I'm legally Brooklyn born, and if I don't say that in front of Corey and Vernon they get pissed off at me"—and raised in a house in Northeast Bronx with his older brother and sister. Calhoun's mother grew up on an organic farm in North Carolina, with a fiercely independent and self-sufficient father (Calhoun's namesake) who lived the ethos that "a free Black man is a man who doesn't have to ask for anything." Calhoun's maternal grandmother was an intelligent and fashionable woman whose example inspired the many educated Black women in Calhoun's family (his mother and sister both hold master's degrees from New York University). His father was a naval sea captain who grew up in Norfolk, Virginia, and traveled the globe for his work, and his mom was a pediatrician and dietician who worked at Brooklyn's Kings County Hospital throughout his childhood.

All the members of Living Colour grew up in the 1960s and 1970s, with the civil rights movement, Black power movement, and Black arts movement on the television and at the dinner table. Political conversations about civil rights, Black liberation, and the profound and enduring contributions of Black peoples to American history and culture swirled, guaranteeing that each of these men would develop a political consciousness at a young age. As Calhoun recounts:

> The house was filled with information on Islam, on Christianity. We had to read Machiavelli. We had to read, in terms of angled stuff, sometimes, you know, Elijah Muhammad's, [*How to*] *Eat to Live* book. These are books that I just remember, like, plopping down at the table, like "read this." You know, I wasn't really into comics and that kind of stuff, so it was interesting for me to read those. And then, of course, [James] Baldwin.

Reid, too, was educated about what it means to be Black in the United States, and he was deeply affected by the political upheaval that he saw on his television set. There were two events that had a profound effect on a young Reid: the 1963 assassination of President John F. Kennedy and the murder of Kennedy's killer, Lee Harvey Oswald, by Jack Ruby on live television. "It was a packed courtroom and I remember it was pandemonium." And he would see other shocking developments on television: "My first experience of Black consciousness was seeing news reports of the civil rights protests and Bull Connor with fire hoses and dogs." Given that these early stirrings of revolution *were* televised, Black Americans' persistent fight for political and social equality were seen and felt by Americans from all racial and ethnic backgrounds. This struggle for change was a constant heartbeat that permeated all parts of life for the families of the young men who would one day find each other in Living Colour. This insistent murmur was reflected in the music of the times—soul, jazz, rock, and other vital American musical styles such as R&B, gospel, and folk—and these potent sounds played a crucial role in the artistic development of Calhoun, Glover, Reid, and Skillings.

Skillings grew up in the same era as his future bandmates. For his family, music was a constant: "My parents hosted gatherings in the home and there was music and dancing. My oldest siblings listened to rock and soul music and R&B, jazz music, hard bop, folk music—which now they call Americana." He also showed exceptional promise as a musician as a young person. "My father put a guitar in my hands when I was five. By the time I was seven, I knew how to play twenty-eight songs. I loved the guitar. I loved the drums. I loved the bass. I was self-taught on the bass, keyboards, and drums." While his parents were not professional musicians, and music—or the prospect of making it a career—was not especially encouraged, Skillings saw music as a regular part of life. It was always there.

A borough away in Brooklyn, Glover was torn between his love of acting and his musical talent. While he began singing in the church at the age of six, he started acting soon after and was a professional actor long before making his mark in rock. Born on November 6, 1964, Glover was raised with an older brother and sister in Crown Heights, a racially mixed neighborhood of working- and middle-class residents. His mother was an elementary school teacher, and his father was a tax assessor for the city of New York. Similar to the other members of Living Colour, music was ubiquitous:

> My brother was the singer in the family and my sister was the actress, so I became both. And they [his parents] encouraged that *a lot*. Maybe a little too much because I had no other options in my life. When I decided to become an actor, my father sat me down and gave me a speech about how the music and how the artist profession is a very tenuous one and that you have to have a fallback plan. You always have to have a fallback plan. And, fortunately, I never took that advice. I tried to have a fallback plan, but it really didn't work.

Rock history would be very different had Glover become the airline pilot he dreamed of being: "I think my fallback plan was more ambitious than me becoming an actor or a singer. . . . It's twice as much work. You know, so that's not a great backup plan." Glover heard great sonic diversity in the home and on the streets as music poured out of New York City windows: "When I was very young, there was a lot of Miles Davis being played, there was a lot of Santana being played, as well as the Beatles and the Stones and that kind of stuff. And not only that. Because where I lived was such a cultural melting pot, I heard music from different places constantly."

Glover's parents were born and raised during the Depression, so they were practical people who knew what it was like to make do with very little. They were also involved in the civil rights movement, and like many other Black folks who came of age in the first half of the twentieth century, they bought into the idea of racial uplift, believing formal education would set their children on the path to social and economic mobility: "So they very much were looking forward to me furthering my education in some way. Even if it was going to be in the arts, then you're going to get an education in the arts."

Calhoun's parents also played a wide range of music in the home, and like Glover, he had older siblings who shared their musical passions and opened new sonic worlds:

> My father was a bebop, jazz Nazi. World Music. My mom was into Leontyne Price and a lot of the gospel greats and blues greats. And of course, they both were into the Harry Belafonte types. . . . And then I'm the youngest of three, so my older brother and sister, when we were young [were musical influences], and then I have an uncle who, thank God, survived the Vietnam war. He introduced me to Sly Stone, Jimi Hendrix Band of Gypsys, Mandrill, War, and early James Brown.

As for Reid's parents, they were enamored with music that spoke to their multiple identities and experiences:

> My parents were very much into Caribbean music, but they were fascinated by American music. And they were huge fans of James Brown and Otis Redding. Joe Tex—

absolutely. I heard a lot of Stax Records and heard a lot of the Motown music. And also, at the same time, because my parents were in London, when the British Invasion bands started happening, I remember my mom was a fan of the Dave Clark Five and stuff like that. The Beatles. I saw the Beatles on *The Ed Sullivan Show*. I remember that. I remember seeing B.B. King show up on television and Johnny Cash. I love Johnny Cash.

Glover's foray into a professional acting career began at fifteen, when he accepted his first serious job as a camp counselor at a day camp in his neighborhood. A small theater company called Acting by Children came to the day camp to put on a production using some of the seven–twelve-year-old campers and fourteen–sixteen-year-old counselors for the cast. Glover was offered a part and traveled with the show across NYC. Acting by Children also had a theatrical management company, and they used these sorts of productions as recruitment tools to find young talent for commercial work. Ultimately, Glover was offered representation, along with two other youngsters, by the management company:

> I became a professional actor at that point. I was doing a bunch of commercials. I think part of the goal, because they heard me sing, was Broadway. If you can sing and you can act and you can dance a little—I was a horrible dancer. I'm still a horrible dancer—But maybe we can get you on Broadway. And I was like "that would be great!"

Glover had early success and booked local and national TV commercials, including an early 1980s ad for the NYC-based Children's Aid Society, which was ubiquitous in the New York Tri-State-Area. He appeared in other spots, too—a Ragu Pizza Quick Sauce commercial with Emmanuel Lewis, an Armed Forces commercial, and a McGruff the Crime Dog commercial. "I was always a sidekick. As most Black men of a certain age were, you know, always the sidekick of somebody." As he continued down his path as an actor, he contemplated his future. While Crown Heights offered vibrancy and diversity, he sensed there was more just across the bridge in Manhattan. As he reached his senior year of high school, he noticed an evolution in his musical tastes that foreshadowed the next steps he would take on his artistic journey: "I went from the pop music of the time, and the burgeoning of hip hop, into hardcore for some reason. And was way into the Brains and Circle Jerks and Leeway and all that stuff." He started attending hardcore matinees at CBGBs, and he would incorporate those hardcore sounds he loved as a teenager into future Living Colour material, most notably "Time's Up."

While Glover was navigating the way to his musical center, Calhoun was falling in love with the drums. His older brother, Charles, was a drumming prodigy who was six years older. There were other young musical talents in the neighborhood who Calhoun looked up to including Ray Chew ("His backyard faced our backyard"), who, at age eighteen, became the musical director for Ashford and Simpson. He then went on to become musical director for "Dancing with the Stars." Drummer Steve Jordan lived three blocks away, and he joined the SNL band in the late 1970s while in his early twenties. Jordan is currently the touring drummer for the Rolling Stones. And hip-hop pioneer Errol "Pumpkin" Bedward was a drummer/multi-instrumentalist band leader who sold beats he created to record labels in the 1970s, long before there was a proper industry for hip-hop, sampling, or looping. Pumpkin lived nearby and would drop by Calhoun's house to hang out with his brother. "I was nine or ten years old, and I saw my neighbors performing on television, or at Madison Square Garden, or on *Soul Train*, so I was exposed to greatness in real time," Calhoun said. The Calhouns owned a two-family home, and they eventually turned the downstairs apartment into a neighborhood rehearsal studio with a "PA system, keyboards, drums, percussion, and guitar and bass amps." Calhoun's brother played music in multiple genres—jazz, gospel, and funk— and with Black, Latin, and White musicians alike. "He told me not to judge White musicians or European-based music; however, know where music comes from. And he brought White guys over to the house to play." When Calhoun was sixteen, the allure of playing in a band, and perhaps one day being on television like his earliest young musician heroes, was strong so he decided to take drum lessons at the Drummers Collective with Horacee Arnold. And before that, while he was very young, he was exposed to music/theory at the Bronx House, a Jewish summer camp and music/art center.

Other members of the band were getting more serious about their love for music around the same time. When Reid was fourteen, he had a fateful conversation about music with his eighteen-year-old cousin, John, who lived in upstate New York. When John discovered how serious Reid was about music, he offered to give him the old guitar he no longer played:

> And then one day, he pulls up the car and he pulls out the guitar out of the case. He pulled it out of the trunk, and it was an acoustic guitar, a Gibson Hummingbird. I had no idea that this was actually a pretty cool Gibson guitar. I knew nothing about the value of it.

Reid continues:

> I had a bike and I would run around with my best friend Lester riding my bike all over Brooklyn. And I rode past this music school. And I decided I wanted to try to take a lesson or something and, also one of the barbers named Melvin, he was an old blues picker. And so he tried to show me a few things. So I had this barber shop guy and also one of my uncles played guitar, but he kind of played in a little combo. But the first couple of lessons it was very hard to hold the strings down, and actually I stopped playing guitar. I kinda quit, but I had the guitar. It was in my room.

But he would soon pick up the guitar again. He played in a variety of bands by age seventeen—from wedding to Top 40—and he was inspired by a range of genres. Joining Ronald Shannon Jackson's jazz and funk improvisational Decoding Society in the late 1970s was the natural next step.

> Even though the music was very different, it was very influential, because he had started out with very, very avant-garde music. He made definitive moves with the

music. Definitive choices in terms of instrumentation. He hired, fired, and kept shaping it. And then, I saw him grow an audience. It wasn't like a stadium one, but he would fill a club. We got to a point where we played the Bottom Line. We played the Montreux Jazz Festival.

In 1984, Reid left the band after having an argument with Jackson in Indonesia when Reid arrived back at the van to go to the next tour stop. While Reid was proud of the music they made and the small, but faithful, fan base they built, he was ready to start his own band, what would become Living Colour.

About two years before this parting, Calhoun was at his own crossroads. In 1982, when it was time to go to college— and this was a given—Calhoun was accepted at New York University, but he decided to attend Berklee College of Music instead. This decision was not automatic. His family wanted him to attend NYU, given that his mother and sister earned advanced degrees there, and there were some jazz legends in the neighborhood who warned Calhoun that he would come out of Berklee sounding like everyone else: "You can't learn music in a school. You know, we're Black. We're Africans. We're African Americans. It's in our DNA. They were telling me there are other ways to learn the music." Others, like his old friend Pumpkin, counseled him differently—"Calhoun, you gotta do it. If it sucks, just come back to the Bronx. But there's nobody from the Bronx that's up there. Maybe you can help us with some information"—and convinced him of the special opportunity. At Berklee, as a compromise for his family, he was a recording and engineering major:

It was beautiful and challenging. . . Berklee was a great environment for focusing on my craft. I practiced very often. I wanted to learn drumming, ear training, harmony, film composing, and more from the best teachers in and out of school. There are frightening drummers, bass players, guitarists, keyboardists, or more, up there to remind you that you're nowhere near the baddest mofo on the block. However, many of the upper-class brilliant players took the time to tutor us newcomers—only if they thought you were promising.

When he graduated, Calhoun's first professional gig was with Harry Belafonte. And later he played with renowned bass player Jaco Pastorius in a trio writing group at the Jazz Cultural Theatre in NY. One night, while he was still at Berklee, he went to see Bushrock, one of his favorite bands, at the 55 Grand club. The rest is history:

Jaco walked past me and said "Hey, Will, what's going on? How's school?" And I said, "It's cool." And then Vernon walked by and he [Jaco] says "Hey, do you know this guy?" And I said, "no, I don't." He says, "You two guys need to meet. You guys need to know each other" . . . . And I said, "Sure, Man," and I met Vernon and that was it.

Later, Calhoun attended a Black Rock Coalition meeting. Calhoun and Reid had the opportunity to have a longer conversation and found that they had a lot in common. They exchanged cassette tapes of each other's bands—Dark Sarcasm and Vernon Reid's Living Colour, respectively—and became fans of each other. During this time, Reid and Greg

Tate had a radio show and they played a Dark Sarcasm song on the air, which Calhoun greatly appreciated, as Capital and Columbia were interested in possibly signing his band. And then in late 1986, Reid called Calhoun to see if he could sit in for drummer J. T. Lewis, who couldn't make a gig at Maxwell's in Hoboken. When Lewis and bassist Carl James left at the end of 1986, Reid invited Calhoun to join Living Colour.

But before that, toward the end of Reid's five-year tenure in the Decoding Society (Reid would leave the band after the next tour, changing his focus to Living Colour), he came home from tour and was invited by his middle sister Jennifer to attend a birthday party on the Upper West Side of Manhattan. As Reid remembers, "she dragged me to this party, and she was like, 'We never do anything. You never hang out. You're coming with me to this party.'" When it was time to sing "Happy Birthday" and blow out the candles, some of the guests scrambled to find Glover. As Reid recounts:

It's the only birthday party I've ever been to, that was filled with people, where only one person sang the song. It was really unusual. And Corey was dating this girl at this time. And they brought out the cake. And he just sang it by himself. He had a beautiful voice. Just great tone. It was a very romantic moment. His vibrato—it's kind of like all of the things that are in Corey's voice in Living Colour. He sang ["Happy Birthday"] as a very sweet ballad. So I didn't know at that time that he could scream and carry on and do all of the things. So I just stepped to him and said, "Man, you have a really great voice." And I had no idea what that would mean, but I took his number.

Reid and Glover lived blocks away from each other and didn't know it. They had to go a borough over to Manhattan to meet. Glover remembers the fateful birthday party similarly, though he suggested that he was feeling anything but romantic toward the girl he had been dating. As Glover remembers:

> It was a girl that I had gone on a couple of dates with. And we had stopped. We weren't even dealing with each other at this point when she called me to say, "Could you come to my birthday party?" I was like, "Okay." And I tried to enlist my friends to come with me. And they're like, "Nope, not coming to this party. There's nothing but trouble at that party. Nope. You're on your own." And I promised that girl, so I showed up by myself.

Glover's natural shyness accompanied him, and he was feeling awkward at the party until the cake was wheeled out. At first, the crowd was going to sing "Happy Birthday," but then the girl stopped everyone and said, "Corey's singing 'Happy Birthday' . . . so I sang 'Happy Birthday.' And after that Vernon came up to me." And then Glover didn't hear from him for a long time. In March or April of 1985, Reid called to say that he was looking for a singer for his band and he wanted to send him some Living Colour music to see what he thought. At this point, Glover had dropped out of college, was living at home with his parents, and was working dead-end jobs to supplement his acting money—orange juice stand in Port Authority, supermarket stock boy. Glover had the chance to hear early renderings of "I Want to Know" and "Funny Vibe."

Glover enjoyed what he heard, and he and Reid, who was also living with his own parents, were close enough to visit frequently while working out songs. Reid told Glover that the job was between him and "another guy" (Mark Ledford, one of Calhoun's Berklee classmates) and the decision would come down to what the band thinks. Reid hired Ledford without telling Glover, but a month or so later called to see if Glover could fill in for Ledford at a gig at CBGBs. Glover happily obliged, and when Ledford finally opted to pursue opportunities as a professional sideman, Glover joined Living Colour.

During the rest of 1985, Living Colour, with Reid on guitar, Glover on vocals, Carl James on bass, and J. T. Lewis on drums, played New York–area shows at venues like CBGBs, Maxwell's, and the Pyramid Club. Meanwhile, Glover auditioned for and got the role of Francis in Oliver Stone's *Platoon*. After accepting the part, knowing he had to leave for the Philippines the following day, he walked over to Reid's house and let him know: "I got good news and I got bad news. Good news is I got a job. Bad news I'm gonna be gone for a minute. Can you hold the fort down while I'm gone? [Reid says] 'Don't worry about it. The gig is still yours. When you get back, we'll get back to it.'"

Whatever glamour Glover thought he might find on the set of *Platoon* was not evident during his three months of "hard labor" in the jungles of Luzon. There were many days where they worked longer than the usual ten to twelve hours, and they didn't have any typical amenities, such as trailers, on set. While Glover was away, long-simmering tensions among band members were coming to the surface. In 1986, the band was still known as Vernon Reid's Living Colour and as Reid's profile as a musician, cultural critic, and cofounder of the Black Rock Coalition continued to rise, bassist and drummer, James and Lewis, respectively, wondered if everyone's contributions were being perceived and celebrated the same way by the public and if the financial rewards matched with the work every band member put in. The latter concern came to a head when Glover was not available to perform at a gig while he was on the *Platoon* shoot. Mark Ledford filled in for Glover, and as Glover recalls:

> Mark did the gig and I think after that gig, the prevailing sort of thoughts were who's benefiting from this? Who gets—I understand if I'm a sideman, you're gonna pay me a particular amount of money to just play my part and do my part. But this thing, this band is a collaborative collective sort of thing, but I don't think we're all getting the benefits of the collaboration. So there was some tension there between them and Vernon.

Shortly thereafter, James and Lewis left Living Colour to tour with Steve Winwood. With a looming show at Maxwell's and two holes in the lineup, Reid invited Calhoun to play, and Calhoun brought along a bass player from the Bronx, Billy Grant. Calhoun's friend did not click with Living Colour's musical aesthetic, but Calhoun was a great fit. After Lewis and James quit, Calhoun was in, but the band still needed a bass player.

In 1986, Skillings was thoroughly enjoying his studies at CCNY:

> I had the good fortune to study some really cutting-edge advanced theory, harmony from some very accomplished teachers. I get the difference between Mozart and Handel now. It's not just classical music. You get to see what a badass Mozart was. Just in context, from back then, you get to see why someone like Beethoven was innovative. And then the difference between him and someone like Tchaikovsky. . . . So I had a very good sense of learning that kind of history, also, especially applying it to jazz. I had the very good fortune to study ragtime, to study jazz, and also, you know, just being inundated with just the r&b of the day and the pop music of the day. But really understanding the importance of African American expression, and how cutting edge it was and what we were doing.

This type of scholarly engagement resonated with Skillings to such a degree that he considered pursuing a Ph.D. Skillings' ethnomusicological and music theory training offered a new perspective on music that positively informed his own work as a sought-after bass player in New York City. And soon Living Colour would find their final bandmate. As Glover recollects, "Bill Toles, one of the executives in the Black Rock Coalition, suggested Muzz. And Muzz came along, and he was a good fit. The four of us fit well—did really well together. Sounded really good together." Skillings saw Living Colour's potential immediately:

> The first rehearsal was like, nobody can stop this. And it was based on my knowledge of what I knew that Blackness

was in terms of expression. That special thing. It was there. Calhoun, I used to call some of the things he would do double dutch. And I don't know if he liked it, but it was like the highest compliment because to me, it was like when I saw girls in my neighborhood doing double dutch, and the rope, and the way they move, and the swinging and motion and when they got in there with a style and the chants that they would say, and the swing that was on it.

Doug Wimbish, the current bass player for Living Colour (Skillings left in 1992 and Wimbish joined that same year), shares similar origins with his bandmates. Born on September 22, 1956, in Hartford, Connecticut, Wimbish, like Reid, has West Indian roots. His mother is from Nassau in the Bahamas (she "didn't know about the situation that was really going down with African American folk up here, because they were coming from the Bahamas—a different vibe over in Nassau"). His father is African American and Native American and was born in Georgia and raised in Bloomfield, Connecticut. His father's migration from the South to the Northeast echoes Calhoun's parents' experience. His father started one of the first social clubs for African Americans in Connecticut, the Esquire Club, and he held a good job at an electrical company. Eventually, Wimbish's mother went to night school and earned a degree at Central Connecticut State College, ultimately becoming a social worker. "That was fortunate to have a mother and father, a stable household, roof over our head. You know, you can't take that for granted. But my family was the kind that the door was always open," Wimbish said.

Wimbish grew up in the 1960s and 1970s listening to rock, Motown, and other types of music, and his eclectic listening tastes led him to eventually becoming a bass player who was open to exploring diverse musical palettes in varied genres. He was keenly aware of the civil rights movement and his father attended the 1963 March on Washington:

> My father and his friends were able to get together, collect money, and when that March on Washington came up, they got a train, they got their own car, out of Hartford, Connecticut, which is unheard of. And got all their friends together, and they raised money to get their own train car to go down to Washington, D.C. He's a photographer. He filmed the March on Washington. So he has that on film. Some of his pieces are in the Connecticut Historical Society.

In much the same way the other members of Living Colour moved between Black and White educational institutions and musical environments, Wimbish took summer classes at the predominantly White Hartford Conservatory where he received classical instruction while simultaneously attending Jackie McLean's Artists Collective, located in a Black neighborhood and which offered applied training. This was the early 1970s and Wimbish was already playing in bands, so this course of study had an immediate practical application. As Wimbish recounts:

> Jackie McLean, the jazz saxophone player, created an artist collective, which was much brighter and much more informative to me. Because it was a collective, this is 1973,

it was music artists, singers, dancers, players, and if you didn't have any money, you could sweep the floor and do a chore and take the lesson. So it was realistic. It was prep school for being a musician. It was understanding how not to be that kid that might have parents you can whine to so they give you a guitar, and next year you're not interested. No, you had to work for it.

From 1974 to 1979, Wimbish worked at All Platinum Records with the soon-to-be legendary godmother of hip-hop Sylvia Robinson and her husband Joe. In 1979, at twenty-three, Wimbish joined the house band for Sugar Hill Records, playing bass on iconic tracks including "White Lines (Don't Don't Do It)" by Melle Mel, "The Message" by Grandmaster Flash and the Furious Five, and "Apache" by the Sugarhill Gang. Wimbish became a highly successful session player working with major acts such as the Rolling Stones, Mick Jagger, Depeche Mode, James Brown, and George Clinton. And during the mid-1980s, Wimbish joined forces with guitarist Skip McDonald and drummer Keith LeBlanc, all veteran members of the Sugar Hill Records House Band, to form the well-regarded industrial hip-hop group Tackhead.

Wimbish met Reid for the first time in 1983 before Reid formed Living Colour. The two musicians would collaborate on different projects, while Reid and Greg Tate played Tackhead on their radio show. Eventually, Wimbish would set the fateful meeting between Mick Jagger and Living Colour in motion during some downtime while working on Jagger's second solo album *Primitive Cool*:

We're at SIR rehearsing and Mick had heard about Living Colour. "Doug, I've been hearing about this band. Blah Blah Blah what do you think?" "They're killing it. As a matter of fact, they're playing at CBGB. Why don't you and Jeff [Beck] go check them out." "Oh, yeah. Okay, cool." So they go down and check out Living Colour. The band knew he was coming in. They were kind of freaking out. Mick comes back the next day, "Dougie? What do you think? I like the band. What do you think I should do?" I'm like, "Man, you're friggin Mick Jagger. You're breaking all these new cats. Why don't you take them in the studio?"

Jagger produced Living Colour's demo, which Ron St. Germain (Bad Brains, Sonic Youth) recorded, and despite facing a great deal of rejection because they were Black men playing rock, they were eventually signed to Epic Records. Released in 1988, *Vivid* was a huge critical and commercial success and Living Colour opened for the Rolling Stones on their *Steel Wheels* tour. When the tour was over, they went back into the studio to begin production on *Time's Up*.

2
"Time's Up"
Time's Up in Their Own Words

Coming off the tremendous critical and commercial success of their debut record, *Vivid*, and after their opening for the Rolling Stones *Steel Wheels* tour that ended in December 1989, Living Colour went back into the studio. In March 1990, Will Calhoun, Corey Glover, Vernon Reid, and Muzz Skillings; producer Ed Stasium; engineer Paul Hamingson; and an assortment of technical personnel, including Glover's vocal coach, Greg Drew, and Reid's guitar tech, Dennis Diamond, began recording the band's second record, *Time's Up*. When the basic tracks were completed in Studio A at the famed A&M Studios in Los Angeles, the production returned to New York City to record overdubs and vocals at RPM Studios, with mixing at Right Track Studio.

Following are excerpts from interviews I conducted in 2014, 2021, and 2022. They have been edited for length and clarity.

Back in the Studio—LA Style

"Studio A is where they did 'We Are the World.'"

Will Calhoun: I felt like we were a little bit on the
hamster wheel because of the Stones tour and
MTV.

Greg Drew: The Stones thing finished pretty close to
Christmas in '89. And by like March, they were
getting ready to make *Time's Up*.

Ed Stasium: A&M has this giant, huge room. Studio A is
where they did "We Are the World." They had two big
isolation rooms where you could partition off the bass
amplifiers and the guitar amplifiers, and a nice vocal
booth. We didn't have all that privilege at Skyline in
New York City with *Vivid*. All that drum stuff that
you hear on *Time's Up* is actually the A&M Studio A
room sound. On "Love Rears Its Ugly Head" that's
just all a live performance, except we overdubbed the
vocals. That was a take.

A New Reality

" . . . that refrigerator over there is basically worth a Lexus."

Paul Hamingson: It takes money to fund the
instruments that it takes to make a record for most
bands. You need to have things that produce the

sound that you're after, that stay in tune, that produce something that's unique in your sound. And then you have to reproduce that night after night on the road. So when we came into *Time's Up*, Will has a huge kit in a big room. There are multiple cabinets on the bass rig. Vernon has a big rack, which I think at one point he pointed to it and said "that refrigerator over there is basically worth a Lexus."

Vernon Reid: I think I'd started working with Mesa Boogie amplification by *Time's Up*. So that changed my tone. That changed the sound. It was less argy-bargy. I mean, you know, the samplers we went from the S900 to the S1000. I was just exploring different things in terms of guitar, in terms of the tech that we used. That was definitely a big change from *Vivid*.

From *Vivid* to *Time's Up*

"Despite the success on the outside, that wasn't what was happening on the inside."

Corey Glover: So we got back to work. Some of those songs were written while we were on the road with the Stones. "Solace of You" was written on the road because we knew at the end of the Stones tour, we got to go into the studio and get some work done. Because if we don't, we were going to miss an opportunity. Despite the success on the outside, that wasn't what was happening on the inside. We were still struggling. We were still working-class. And we couldn't get rid of that idea. That's not something we can ever get rid of. You cannot get rid of the fact that even if you were brought up middle-class, or even if you were brought up with some sort of privilege as African American men, and people in general, you still got to work hard for what you get. We have decided that we're gonna have to work really hard at this.

Vernon Reid: We were charged with, and burdened on a certain level with, a feeling of responsibility that we couldn't half-step. That's a kind of oppressive state to be in. The idea that something has to be important is its own reaction to trauma.

Muzz Skillings: *Vivid* paved the way for *Times Up*. Like in the business sense, and in just a record label dynamic sense and the corporate sense, the success of that record and everything we brought to it paved the way for the second record. It set the tone and made it possible. But knowing that, you know, I wasn't interested in building off of or continuing *Vivid* in any way. Our audience had grown. It grew exponentially from the time of *Vivid*'s release to when we were starting to record *Time's Up*. The only thing on my mind that I was interested in was resonating with this new expanded audience. That was my goal. It was amazing and a blessing that they were there.

Corey Glover: *Vivid* made a statement. We had more to say. And we felt like if we didn't make another statement, we'd be stuck living in this little bubble. So we would talk about love as well as what one might call social issues.

Will Calhoun: We wanted it to sound fucking incredible, and we wanted our musicianship to be high, and we wanted the impact to be challenging and earth shattering. We didn't want people to just sit down and drink wine to the record. We wanted people to think about it.

Paul Hamingson: They had presented quite a lot to the world and got back a lot from the world on that first one. And that shaped the second one. It shaped the way that they were able to play. There's a difference between a band that's been on the road playing for a year in front of different audiences and what they can produce when you put them in a room.

Ed Stasium: From the moment we started rehearsing, I had a concept. I think the guys had a concept. We didn't want to duplicate what had been done with *Vivid*. This turned into, as I called it, the Black Sgt. Pepper. It has a flow to it. We have all these soundscapes. Vernon had gone into, with his effects, all the different deep African roots and reggae roots and Afro-Caribbean stuff. And we do have the heavy rock stuff, but everything is intertwined with the soundscapes. Every song flows into each other starting off with "Time's Up" with those clocks.

"Time's Up"

"I wanted to do a punk rock song my whole life."

Will Calhoun: "Time's Up" was deep because we were
probably talking about the Bad Brains, I think,
sonically; yet Corey had this idea, which, ironically,
now is, you know, it's like climate change in 1990!
We talked about these kind of things. And we said,
how can we put this Bad Brains energy into a climate
change song? And then, have it be provocative? And
then he went between the funk part and a really fast
flash part, and that song was quickly assembled once
we had the concept. Sometimes we throw things
out to challenge ourselves. We don't always win. But
sometimes you get dealt a nice hand. Sometimes
we can say, hey, what about if we put this idea with
this? And sometimes it doesn't come out so great.
But "Time's Up," it came out amazing. It's actually my
favorite song to this day to play live.

Muzz Skillings: You have artists—musical artists,
referring to us. You have artist as mirror, right? You
have artist as town crier. You have artist as provocateur.
We were always all three, but with varying degrees of
emphasis with each mode. Sometimes the music would
be in one of those modes, while the lyrics would be
purely in another. Listen closely and you'll be able to
hear what I mean. When we created the song, it was at
a much faster tempo than what you hear on the record.
We slowed it down thinking it would have a better

feeling. The funny thing is we ended up playing it much faster live anyway.

Corey Glover: I wanted to be a punk rock singer. I wanted to do a punk rock song my whole life. This is my opportunity to do a punk rock song. You're only gonna get one take. It's what it is. What's there is there. I literally left. I left the building. Because the door out of the studio was closer to the vocal booth than it was to the control booth, I went out of the vocal booth and down the stairs and out the building.

Greg Drew: And everybody thought he was going to the bathroom. Ten minutes later, I'm sitting out in the lounge probably watching the basketball game with Will Calhoun and they come out like, "Where's Corey?" I said, "He left." "What do you mean he left? We're working on 'Time's Up.'" I said, "He said he was gonna sing it once," and they kind of look at me.

Vernon Reid: "Time's Up" was very much meant as an homage to the Bad Brains. That one segment, I want to do something kind of fast and hard and want to do something that was just aggressive and kind of played around and Corey came up with these lyrics that were like, "Time's Up. The rivers have no life." I go, "Let's go with that," but he [Corey] had this whole environmental thing, which was, not talking about the man or talking about the vampires or whatever, but it was really about the planet. So it's kind of like a hardcore tune about the planet. And I thought this is so different than what I would have expected. "The forest, the trees, the rivers, the seas, all die of this disease." That's phenomenal.

"History Lesson"

"All the ambitions I had for this piece that I was working on."

Vernon Reid: "History Lesson" is actually an excerpt. Oh my Lord have mercy. All the ambitions I had for this piece that I was working on. I had gotten a grant from the public access synthesizer studio and I was working on a piece that was turned into an excerpt of a longer theatrical piece I never finished called "Afrerika." And it was about the absurdity of race and somebody going on a journey, a metaphysical journey through Blackness, through the conflicts about what it meant to be Black. It was probably influenced by Lewis Carroll and *The Green Pastures*, which is one of the great weird movies of all time.

Ed Stasium: That was a Vernon solo piece. That's all Vernon. . . . There's other speakers on there besides James Earl Jones. And there are bits and pieces that are lifted from an African record, a field recording, maybe?

"Pride"

"It's just a massive sound."

Will Calhoun: A lot of lyrics from "Pride" came from me digging through my notes from junior high school. I was packing some things, and I stumbled across some old poems and things. And I took a few lines from my high school ramblings, and I put those lyrics together, wrote verses around two things: my experience being in the band and some things the press wrote—"Why you guys play rock?"—a combination of that and how we were viewed, and what it was like for me to be a young African American guy and know what I know and be who I am. And how people just had a hard time with it.

Corey Glover: "Pride" was primarily Will's tune. Will wrote most of that song. That's his baby. And again, this is from lived experience. We—I completely related to that song. I understood that song really really well, so doing it was easy.

Vernon Reid: That's like Will Calhoun's take on a kind of Van Halen type of tune. He's a big Van Halen fan. And when I think of that tune, that's almost like a Van Halen-esque type of riff. And then the other thing is I *love* the chorus of this tune. "History's a lie that they teach you in school/A fraudulent view called the golden rule." I love that chorus because it's also true.

Greg Drew: There's a tricky little interval that, of course, Mr. Calhoun had put in the song in the melody that Corey didn't always hit. In fact, in the MTV thing [MTV New Years 1990 Show], being a vocal coach, I hear the little bit that he didn't quite always nail, pitch-wise. And it was just because it was a real odd combination of notes. He and I talked about it, and we actually came up with an exercise where he would do those notes over and over, up and down the scale. We called the exercise

Calhouns in honor of Will. We did that maybe four or five days before it was time to do that vocal on "Pride." And so when he went to do it, it was second nature.

Ed Stasium: Will's massive drum playing. BOOM. That comes closest to "Cult of Personality" in vibe more than any other song on this particular record . . . it's just a massive sound.

"Love Rears Its Ugly Head"

"Yeah, all of us had been in that dating situation where it kind of sneaks up on you."

Vernon Reid: "Love Rears Its Ugly Head" is the companion tune to "Broken Hearts" from the first album, and weirdly enough, these two songs are about the same woman. In "Love Rears Its Ugly Head," it was about falling in love with this person. And "Broken Hearts" is about breaking up with this person. And you know, the thing about it was I really didn't want to be in a relationship. I was like, I've been burned by this thing and then I—that's why they call it falling in love right? It's like the next thing you know, you're waiting for the phone to ring and you're hoping that it's her. We actually used to do that as a kind of mid-tempo tune. And then I said, we should slow this down to like a Sly Stone type of vibe. I said it wasn't working at this tempo, and I said we need to slow this down, and that's when it finally worked.

"Love Rears Its Ugly Head" was the hit single off of *Time's Up*. That was the song. That was the most popular song in Europe and the UK.

Greg Drew: When we were out in LA, there was a young lady who thought the best way to get to Corey Glover's heart was to just smother him. And after a time, it was having the opposite effect that she desired. And they used to take phone messages out at the desk at A&M studios. And if you happen to go out into the lobby, they would say, "Oh, here are messages for Studio A." And one of them was from this young lady, and it said, "Corey, please call me." And so I brought it back in, and I showed it to him, and he kinda rolled his eyes. And that night, as we're packing up to leave, he's already left, and I noticed that the piece of paper was still there. This was in the pre-electronic days, so I actually had a folder with song lyrics and exercises and things like that. So I just stuck it in the folder and thought that it would be useful at some point in the future. And so when it came time to record "Love Rears Its Ugly Head," they had a music stand that they would put out where the microphone was, and they would tape the lyrics to the music stand. And so I went out and taped the little phone message next to the lyrics. And so when Mr. Glover walked out into the studio and saw that he just started laughing. And he said, "I'm ready now." And he pretty much sang the song down from beginning to end. (Laughs) And he told me afterward that I put him in the proper mood.

Corey Glover: Yeah, all of us had been in that dating situation where it kind of sneaks up on you and really could relate. Vernon wrote the lyrics and when we played it, at the end of the song, I would lose my shit, just like this. This is me, completely losing my mind. And under the realization that I am, that I have just fallen in love and didn't know it. And I thought that was very funny. It was fun to do. I remember having a hard time with the timing of certain things like entrances and exits and certain things. Like the second verse: When do I come in here? That was going on with "Love Rears." It's a blues tune. I was trying to be as blues singer as I possibly could. Not an R&B singer. Not a rock singer. But a blues singer.

Ed Stasium: There's a couple samples that we used from "Funny Vibe." I'm standing by the wedding march— Funny Vibe! That's Muzz and we used that on "Funny Vibe" on the first record. We kept that and actually I think Will had that sample in one of his syndrums. It was a sampler that he would hit and that would come up. And also the BAAM that horn hit. We use that also somewhere on the first record. I don't remember where. It might have been "Funny Vibe."

"New Jack Theme"

"David Dinkins was sitting in the audience, and he was not amused."

Vernon Reid: The thing was kind of like mixing metal with house music. That was the idea and it kind of worked. We played that at the Grammys. We got a Grammy for *Time's Up*. And we played that and "Crack is the master. I am a New Jack" and David Dinkins [NYC's first Black mayor] was sitting in the audience, and he was *not* amused. You know, it's about this dealer and he's not apologizing. "I make more money than a judge or a cop/Give me a reason why I should stop."

Corey Glover: It was like a house music tune, but old-school house music, like Larry Levan house music. That's what it felt like to me. I wasn't trying to sound like Sylvester, but I *was* trying to sound like Sylvester. I was trying to sing like Corey sounding like Sylvester. I wasn't gonna do the falsetto stuff, but I was gonna do it as high in my register as I possibly could and keep that sort of like bounce to it.

Ed Stasium: The intro to that was just an amazing soundscape, conceived and played by Mr. Reid. I remember him sitting in that little room and there's some pictures of him with his rig, and just looking for sounds. He would sit in there for hours when we're doing stuff, setting up drums, whatever. He would get in there before we all would. He'd be experimenting with getting sounds and he came up with some amazing stuff. The soundscape that opens up "New Jack Theme" is just incredible. And also a contributor to that was a fellow named Alan Friedman. He was an assistant at Right Track Studio where we mixed the record, and he came out with all the little samples that he programmed into the reel. We gave him a B reel to listen to and to work with, and he went and did all those samples on his own. He was just a kid. He was an assistant engineer. And I knew that he was doing that stuff. All the programming and the sequencing stuff on there, that's all Alan. He did a great job on that.

"Someone Like You"

"I believe that there's always room for a change that will better the entire situation."

Muzz Skillings: With regards to the chorus of "Someone like You," I wanted to have the same words sung for each chorus. Even though the words were exactly the same, I wanted the words of the chorus to have a different meaning each time you heard it, suggesting a different course of action each time. I wanted each verse to tell a different story. Each story complete within itself, concluding with the chorus as containing a solution, but leaving it up to the listener's imagination of exactly what the solution I'm referring to is. It could be peaceful—talking about the solution—loving, progressive, or not. It could be something entirely different from that. I know what it is. I just don't know if it's prudent or responsible to say. I always intended for whatever I expressed to have a prescriptive component, for example, in the song when it says, "It's never too late to change your ways." I believe that there's always room for a change that will better the entire situation. Like for each individual, whatever role they're playing in, whatever scenario we're talking about, there's always room for every individual to take one step because that's usually how we have to do it as humans. It's usually just one step at a time. The double edge to that is "It's never too late to change your ways," meaning a common criticism is "Black folks, we get oppressed and what do we do? We sing songs. We're full of love. We're peaceful. Where has that gotten us?" It's that mentality, which frankly I don't really think it's prudent to propagate. I think we should stay this course. Not for any ideological reasons. Just for practical reasons. If we were to take other kinds of action en masse, then there may be other repercussions that we may or may not be ready to deal with. When I say it's never too late to change your ways, I'm also talking to people on the other side of the problem. On the bad side of the problem. Saying the way you're handling it, it's not too late the change how you're gonna deal with this. You wanna take it straight to 'em, maybe that's the way. Or if you want to pray for them, maybe that's the way. But either way, it's never too late to change that way as well.

Paul Hamingson: That was Muzz's song, I remember. I think we ended up spending time focusing on making sure that the bass is right on everything, but

I think we probably spent a little extra love on that one. The way that we were doing it at that point was the bass is usually recorded with the drums. And then you'll typically, if there is a note or two out, you'll go back and just when you're set up right then, you'll go right after that and punch in. So just go into record, get a note, and a couple notes or phrase, and then come back out. So it's not like you just set up and get everything ready to record and you don't touch it. That's always a battle between, you know, do I get it more perfect? Or do I preclude the use of that particular take? Like if you made the change between takes, you can't necessarily take one part from one take and another if the tone is drastically different.

Ed Stasium: The playground in the beginning of that was recorded around the corner from my home. Did I have my DAT machine? I must have or I might have used a Walkman. It was probably a cassette. And there's a playground around the corner from my apartment on 78th Street. We wanted to do something unusual for the intro and I don't know who —could have been Muzz— who thought of the playground. But it just happened. I just kind of incognito recorded a bunch of Black kids in there. That was kind of a magical coincidence.

Muzz Skillings: My intention was to have the intro with the sound of the children playing appeal to the listener's humanity. It was meant to convey: "My God! How can they do this to *children*!"

"Elvis Is Dead"

"You're not going out of human memory, as long as you exist in memory to someone."

Vernon Reid: "Elvis Is Dead" was really about the tabloids and was not directed at Elvis. It was directed at the cult around Elvis. And that Elvis didn't die. And Elvis lives. "The tabloids scream that Elvis was seen at the shopping mall." And it was about the absurdity of Elvis will never die, because there are really two deaths, right? There's the death that you have when you die. And then there's a death when the last person that speaks your name, when that person dies, then you're really gone. You're not going out of human memory as long as you exist in memory to someone.

Ed Stasium: I love this song for many reasons. It's got a great groove. It's funky. And it's got the great guest artists on it. It just has all these little bits and pieces. You have the song. Then you have the breakdown. It's a hilarious song. "Picture a zombie Elvis in a tacky, white jumpsuit." And it's a Vernon song. "When the King died, he was all alone/I heard that when he died he was sitting on his throne/Alas, poor Elvis, you made us know you well/Now you'll dwell forever in the heartbreak hotel." It's almost as funny as a Ramones song. "A Black man taught him how to sing," which is true.

Corey Glover: I hated it. I thought it was a dumb song. At first. I thought it—the sentiment was really good.

I didn't like it at first. And then it's like, it's a James Brown tune. Oh, oh, right. Okay, got it. Let's do it. It took me a minute to figure out why it worked. And I was like, I don't want to put the song on the record. It's James Brown. I get it now.

Will Calhoun: I didn't like it. I didn't think it was necessary to talk about that on that record. We already had dope stuff on the record. And I was like, why are we talking about Elvis is dead? So he's dead, but why are we reminding people of that? We talked about Elvis, how we felt about Elvis versus Big Mama Thornton, and so many other people, in our interviews. It didn't move me to be on the record. And then when the Little Richard thing came up and Maceo, and Little Richard being able to make the testified statement that he made on the recording, he *really* put it in a different place. If we just would have played the song without those two guys, I would have vetoed that song.

Greg Drew: The other part I was there for was when they did the thing in the middle where it breaks down. I was there when they did that. And what was cool about that was Will Calhoun sort of directed that. A lot of times, the drummer's the drummer. But Will, because of his background from Berklee, and just his overall musical genius, he always saw the big picture. And so they were adlibbing things. And he was sort of "no no, you do that." "You keep doing that." Just watching them put that section together over the course of a half hour or forty minutes was amazing.

They turned on the microphones, and they all just sort of started saying things. So that was very cool.

Guest Appearances on "Elvis Is Dead"

"Oh, shit. I'm in a room with Little fucking Richard!"

Paul Hamingson: I remember when Maceo came through because that's a highlight. He was such a gentleman. He was such a professional as a musician. And he came through and played it a couple times and that was it. He's that good that he can listen to stuff, understand what their arrangement is, get the bit, and put it on tape. And what an amazing tone.

Ed Stasium: I did not record the Little Richard vocal. I don't even know who recorded that. I don't even think it's credited. They did it at A&M Studios when we were in New York. We had met Little Richard at his suite. I guess it was at the time it was still the Continental Hyatt House. I get so nervous when I'm meeting people that I admire. I can't even tell you. Working with Jagger, my hands were always sweating. But Little Richard—I just remember going into his dark suite at the hotel and just being there smiling, going "Oh, shit. I'm in a room with Little fucking Richard!"

Vernon Reid: It was wild. He [Little Richard] came in [to A&M Studios in Los Angeles] and he knocked it right out . . . . I was there. It was exciting. He was quick too!

I think first or second take, tops. . . . Our managers looked up his [Maceo's] management and made the request, and he was like, "Man, sure. You know, they must pay my fee" and again, he came in and just knocked it out. One take, baby.

Corey Glover: I was in the room [with Little Richard]. Vernon was in the room. I think all of us were exhausted. We heard that he's not singing. He didn't want to sing along to the chorus. He wanted to do this rap thing. Gotcha. That makes sense. (laughs) That's exactly what we needed. And it worked.

Meeting Little Richard

"He's about six foot three and *I'm not*"

Corey Glover: So I'm hurrying up [on the way to a Grammy party] and I get dressed and I'm running out of my room. I get to the elevator bank and I press a button, and ding ding the door opens up and I walk headfirst into Little Richard. Who's not little. He's about six foot three and *I'm not*, and he looks down at me and says, "Who are you?" "Hi, my name is Corey," I said. "I'm running late. Are you going down?" "Yes, I am." So I get on an elevator with Little Richard. And he's asking me all kinds of questions. I can't answer any of them because I don't know what the hell's going on. It's like, I'm in the elevator with Little Richard. This is weird. It's the weirdest shit ever. It was, "Yes,

Sir. Yes, Sir. No, Sir. No, Sir. Yes, Sir." Finally get to the lobby. Get into the car: "I just had the weirdest interaction with Little Richard just now. Little Richard lives here?" Then I was told, "Yeah, he lives there. He's been living there for the last ten, twelve years. . . . He has a suite up on the top floor." Whatever. Anyway, that's it. That was the most rock and roll thing ever.

Vernon Reid: Well, the thing about getting Little Richard was that we were staying at the Hyatt, which is gone now, but then the pink Hyatt on Sunset, which was the legendary rock and roll hotel famous for destruction of TVs and other things. He had a suite of rooms. He lived at the Hyatt on Sunset. And he had his parlor. Somehow, Little Richard found Corey's room and called him. And he called all of us. And he [Corey] was like, "I ain't going into Richard's room by myself." And so we went in, and it was . . . frankincense was burning in the dark, you know what I mean? And there were several handsome young men just hanging out. It was very much a consultation with the shaman of rock and roll.

Will Calhoun: Most of what he told me I can't share because too many people are still alive! But I will say this about what he wanted us to know: not to look for pats on the back or sanctioning from this industry or from this country. I can say that in a roundabout way, he wanted us to know what certain things people are *not* going to be for y'all. Therefore, you're going to have to do the following: you have to stick to your guns. You're gonna know that the acknowledgement comes from the family, comes from us.

"Type"

"It's really about America."

Vernon Reid: I had a friend, Craig Street. The producer
Craig Street's first wife was named Colette. And
Colette is a fabulous woman. *Very* French. *Very*
cosmopolitan. And we were all in the back of a
cab, coming from Uptown and heading downtown.
And the city was just *full on*. Colette looked out
the cab and she said, "I love New York. Everything
is possible and nothing is real." And that stuck in
my head. I was like, "Yeah, you right. Sure, you
right." It's really about America. It's about the cities.
All the cities are a cornucopia of possibilities, but
are the possibilities possible? It's a song about all
these contradictory things: "Corporate Religion."
"Televangehypnotism."

Paul Hamingson: At some point, the band came to me
and said, "Hey, listen, we're going to go see a band
tonight. You want to come with us?" "Yeah, sure. Who
is it?" They're like, "Oh, we're going to see Rush. We
love Rush." They were huge Rush fans. So they went
and one of the pictures I have of Vernon he's wearing
[a Rush shirt]. So it would have been *Presto*, the *Presto*
tour, and we went and saw them and then got to go
backstage. And they talked to the band for a little bit.
We were in LA, Rush was there, and I think Eddie
and Alex from Van Halen were backstage as well. And

there was a little bit of potential rivalry going at that point.

Dennis Diamond: One night we broke early because we were invited to see Rush play. I can't remember exactly what arena they played in. So it was like "Okay, who invited us? Oh, Rush invited us? Yeah, we're not going to say no. We're breaking early tonight." So we went and saw that. It was inspiring because I think they took a lot of what they saw that night with them. Brought that energy with them in the studio the next day. And so they were knocking out songs like crazy.

Ed Stasium: That's Muzz doing the talking in the background as Corey's saying, "Well, don't think twice." It's like this distorted modulate voice going on. That's Muzz. This ends side one of the vinyl and gives us a little intermission—a little breathing room on the CD. Like I said, this record was made for listening all the way through. It was made for CD. We had that in mind when we were mixing it. How long is it anyway? I don't know. Close to an hour, probably somewhere around there. Fifty minutes or so. And so you have your nice long fade out on "Type."

Corey Glover: "Type" was fun to sing because of the words. The words were great to sort of string together. Vernon wrote those lyrics. But it was my debut as a guitar player on the song, too. I played a little guitar, which I was more excited about than singing. Like fuck singing. I want to play guitar! So of the three chords I knew I played two of them on the song. I was like, yeah, I got a credit as a guitar player now. I can play guitar. That's what I most remember about it.

Muzz Skillings: "Type" was interesting for me. Because it presented a sonic problem, if you will, where the guitar and the bass line are identical. So often, because of reasons I won't go into, the bass would end up not being heard so much. It would be masked excessively, so I knew that going into the second record. So I just invented a solution. So what I did was, I used my Eventide harmonizer H3000B and the TC Electronic 2290 together. Got into it. It's an amazing effects unit. Basically, the song was created with five tracks of bass. In fact, most of the album has five tracks of bass, two stereo effects, you know, chorus, reverb, little bit of delay, and two amp signals. Not stereo amp, but two separate bass amplifier signals, each delayed enough milliseconds to create the Haas effect, which is when you perceive that you're hearing stereo, when it's not really there, but the brain tricks itself. When you know how to use the Haas effect to effect, you can do that. So that's what I did, just to make sure the bass was more enveloping. And then it was just a direct signal, the straight mono signal where you get the meat of the sound from. So I had that going and I forget the name of the patch, but it made the bass almost sound like it was in a room so you can hear it in each ear. And you could feel it, the warmth of it. It was just a really good sound.

"Information Overload"

"It sounds like a computer gone bad, but it's musical."

Vernon Reid: It's like our other song that's a tribute to Rush. Some of the parts are from a certain time period of Rush, and it showed up in "Desperate People" in the first record, and it shows up a little bit in "Information Overload." I think about the beginning of "Information Overload," and the thing I did on this guitar was using this kind of Eventide. I think I was using an H3000 harmonizer, which had this kind of program that scrambled, literally scrambled, the guitar signal, and when I heard it, I said, this sounds like a computer having a nervous breakdown. And I'd never heard anything quite like it. And that was the perfect sound for the beginning of "Information Overload." It was completely bonkers. Nobody had even heard anything quite like it. It's very dense and then it just goes into that first big G chord.

Paul Hamingson: There was a lot of stuff going on in that. That was a ton of soundscape overdubs. Guitar soundscapes in terms of what Vernon was doing on that. I think the basics were fairly straight ahead on pretty much all of these, but the overdubs on that one, there was more painting with sound.

Corey Glover: Again, this is sort of like industrial house. It felt like to me. So I was trying to get that kind of thing. And you know what this whole record was like, we wanted to explore other sounds of it, and mix it in with rock and roll and funk. So this is sort of like the industrial sort of thing that we wanted. We did it again with "Auslander" on the next record, but we were really trying to deal with some harder, more electronic sounds on that.

Ed Stasium: It sounds like a computer gone bad, but it's musical. The genius of Vernon Reid. Two different things going on left and right. . . . We're working on tape. Of course, you could do a lot of stuff digitally now to emulate these effects, but there's something on the tape machines called a varispeed. We can turn on the varispeed and you could speed it up or slow it down. And I've used this—I've incorporated this on quite a few effects on records. Vernon is doing some noise. And while he punched in the last chord there, and while he was doing that, I gradually sped up the machine. I sped it up so when you play it back at normal speed, it actually sounds like it's slowing down. That's what's on the guitars there at the end. And Corey is just normal.

"Under Cover of Darkness"

"I was trying to make a song about safe sex sexy. I don't know if I succeeded."

Vernon Reid: "Under Cover of Darkness" is a song that we all put together. Those lyrics are Corey. It's talking about the clandestine life at a point in your life when you are concerned with sensual things. There's a certain amount of struggling with identity about what desire is: "And I want to feel you. The real you./Not the projection that you let me see."

Corey Glover: I knew folks who worked with Latifah. Friends of mine. I know a lot of rappers. I grew up with a lot of these folks. And I thought Lau was at that time, was the most prolific, very thoughtful, very informed. Very, what we call it today, very woke. And she was the first choice of people to do it. Because, like I said, we knew a lot of rappers, but I wanted to get a female perspective, versus what I was thinking. And Latifah was it for me. I called some friends who called some friends who called her and asked if she wanted to do it. And she wrote those lyrics on the spot. She was incredible. I've known Doug [Wimbish] for a long time. I've known Doug before I was in Living Colour. And she had a relationship with Doug Wimbish as well, to help out a little bit with that.

Ed Stasium: And she [Latifah] was nothing but a sweetheart. She went out there, rehearsed it once, and then nailed it. No dropping and no punching. Just did her thing, sure that she had talked to Vernon and Corey about what she was going to do, and she just put it all together. It was beautiful. And Vernon was used to having his loud guitar, distorted tones for solos, and on this he went to his jazz roots.

Corey Glover: I was trying to make a song about safe sex sexy. I don't know if I succeeded.

"Ology"

"I became keenly interested in creating sounds of unknown origin, and having those sounds be musical to whomever might be listening."

Muzz Skillings: I used to layer my bass on recordings when all I had was a bass guitar and the Univox Micro Rhythmer. I would bounce back and forth between the two tape decks that I had and after that, I got what was called a TEAC Syncaset, which enabled me to do doubletracking without having to bounce back and forth. Then I got a Portastudio four track by Tascam, four track cassette, which was amazing for me. I would create songs where all the instruments were done on the bass. I would use different physical properties of my bass guitar to create different sounds. Some of the sounds were imitative of known instruments like rhythm guitar, kick and snare on the drum, lead guitar, horns, percussion, even vocal melody lines. Some of the sounds were not connected to any known instrument. I became keenly interested in creating sounds of unknown origin, and having those sounds be musical to whomever might be listening. Or whoever might be hearing them. "Ology 1" was born of that intention.

Ed Stasium: There's a loop of some kind on there of Will's. Yeah, that's a crazy ending [to "Under Cover of Darkness"]: "You know you in a mess!" That's some preacher. I don't know who that is. Some sample that

Vernon found somewhere. Then all of a sudden, some wacky drum fill and then that's all Muzz playing all the parts on the bass. It was nice to have these little refreshing bits and pieces. The three of them: "History Lesson," "Ology," and then "Tag Team Partners" mixed in within the realm of the cinemascope recording here. That's all Muzz doing his thing. All different tones. You would never know that that's all bass. There's a drum loop in there, but it's all bass. No guitars at all.

Corey Glover: Muzz had this riff and this run that he was trying to work with, and create something out of, and it turned out beautiful.

"Fight the Fight"

"Every aspect of my life has been in a struggle to change the system."

Corey Glover: I've been dealing with this kind of activism about my rights and about other people's rights since I was a kid. Every aspect of my life has been in a struggle to change the system. And why are we doing that? I just know that as long as I live I'm going to be in some sort of struggle. I'm going to be in a fight. And that's what that song was about. And that's what I was trying to convey.

Vernon Reid: Oh, yeah. "Fight the Fight" is about conflict. My favorite bit of that is the little kind of intro and I kind of love that. This is kind of a co-write, but I think Corey did quite a bit of the lyrics. "We all fight the same fight/We all are in the same war/We all are in the same revolution. We got to know what we're fighting for." Yeah, all that's Corey. I think I do "War is Hell/Peace is Hell/Love is Hell/ What the Hell?" And the funny bit of it is, is that my first wife makes a cameo. When she goes, "I have had it with you!" it turned out that that shit was *really* true. (Laughs)

Muzz Skillings: Okay, so "Fight the Fight." It was a case of instant composition, which is different from pure improvisation. Instant composition follows or adheres to the rules of good composing. You have a particular set of rules that you are going to adhere to. You just do it instantly. The opening bass motif, you know, Vernon, he just hit the chord: "dummm." And I went, "ba dum ba dum ba dum ba dum ba dum dum." And he went, he went to the four chord: "dummm." And I went "ba dum ba dum ba dum ba dum ba dum dum." He went to the minor two chord. And I went to say, "Well sure, ba dum ba dum ba dum ba dum" back to the tonic and then I instantly figured out that the same motif on the bass went to each chord with enough tension and release to make it very interesting for me, just as a composer. It's like, yeah that's really cool. And so that's just one example. "Fight the Fight" is an expression involving advanced music theory, advanced harmony, and a bit of radicalism, taking known rules and convention and purposefully stretching them beyond recognition, but never losing the feeling, which resonates with us as a band, and then our audience.

"Tag Team Partners"

"It takes me back to double dutch."

Corey Glover: It was just me and Doug E. fucking around. It was all completely improv. Yeah, like, just play the track. Like, Doug do something and I do something and Doug do something and I do something. Doug do something, I do something, and mix all together and see what happens.

Paul Hamingson: This was more of an interlude than a bigger set piece on the record. They explored things in terms of how do you tie things together? How do you weave it together so that the album has a continuity to it? Some people are just like I'm gonna write twelve songs, ten of them are going on the record, and I'm gonna figure out how to put them in order. And that's it. And some people make records that have a higher level of cohesion. And I think in going back and listening to this one, they did that a little bit more in this.

Vernon Reid: I just thought it was really cool that Doug E. Fresh kind of came through. And it's a cute piece. And I love the title of it. I love the title of "Tag Team Partners" because it takes me back to the park. It takes me back to double dutch. And there's something very innocent about it. It lends itself to this idea of a narrative, if you will, this aspect of journaling. It took me back to really what we were like—when we were playing Chinese handball and stickball and stuff like that.

"Solace of You"

"And initially the idea was that though you're not here, you're still with me."

Corey Glover: Vernon and I were both influenced by some of the music coming out of South Africa at the time. And it's like, can we find a way to do sort of like the Soweto swing kind of thing, but this was our initial sort of idea. Can we make this jump-up music but say something very poignant like that, and I was saying this in the midst of all this stuff. Before things started to go really crazy my father passed away. We were in Europe around '87 or something and he got sick. And by the time I went back home, and we were back out on the road, he had passed away. And initially the idea was that though you're not here, you're still with me. It was initially what I was writing. Someone comforts you in the worst and the best of times and that's what's important. That's what's part of your growth. Initially, like I said, it was gonna be about my dad, but I was like, no, it's about me growing because of my dad. And that was much more important than just saying, "I'm sorry you're gone. You're not gone. I'm here, so you're not gone." Coupled with all the stuff about apartheid that was still sort of in its last gasps at that point. And I was writing that and sort of tried to make a correlation between the two: my own personal thing and the world.

Greg Drew: In the time between LA and New York, Corey had taken ten or twelve days off. So when he came back to do the first vocal, it wasn't as good as the "Elvis Is Dead" and "Love and Happiness" that he had done out in Los Angeles. We're halfway through the first vocal and Ed turned and looked at me and said, "Why doesn't he sound like he did out in LA?" I said, "Well, he's taken ten days off." And he said, "Is it going to get any better today?" And I said, "probably not. . . . Give me four or five days and we'll get back in shape." And that's what we did.

Paul Hamingson: I'm trying to remember which guitar 'cause that's a really beautiful guitar figure on that. And I seem to think that was one of the Hamers, and I can't remember whether it was the black and white Yin Yang one. I don't think it was the Gibson at that point. There would have been half a dozen or a dozen guitars around.

Dennis Diamond: If you listen real close, you'll hear kind of a beatboxing that sounds like African drums. That's Doug E. Fresh.

Greg Drew: We're hanging out and so he [Corey] said, "we'll think about maybe doing it again." We happen to be watching MTV, and the Sinead O'Connor "Nothing Compares 2 U" video came on, the one where there's close ups of her, and she's got tears running down, you know that one. And I started pointing at the TV: "More like that! More that." There's this thing where singers do the thing where it's like a megaphone going out. And they're spraying the audience with a hose. And there's the other thing where it's like you're bringing the audience in, like you're giving them a big hug. . . . And he was starting to get very emotional as he was singing it ["Solace of You."] And at that point, it was a question of whether we could get the vocal down before he was losing it. And we got it. Ed turned to me and said something like, "I'm so glad we did this. That was great." And as far as I was concerned, those two songs at the end of the record made the whole record. Those two songs are a lot of people's favorite songs on the record.

Ed Stasium: Greg [Drew] was great with Corey. What an amazing singer. After he [Corey] did his vocal he came in the control room in tears. That's never happened to me. Hasn't happened before. Never happened since. And it was a one-take vocal, and it was a beautiful thing. Very rarely do we get one-take vocals. I think I might have mentioned "Midnight Train to Georgia" by Gladys [Stasium was the engineer for this song] was a one-take vocal. And it's very rare that you get those kinds of things.

Vernon Reid: "Solace of You" came out of being backstage. We were on tour. And we were in a dressing room. And I think that was the process of just kind of playing around with it. A kind of quasi-African on guitar figure. And then, you know, chords came with these beautiful words, there was this kind of sequence. There was sort of a kind of crossing, a South African guitar thing and really house music on a level. But kind of folky. It's actually one of the most requested songs for Living Colour. People really love it.

"This Is the Life"

"We're at that age where we're starting to lose parents, you know, this is the life you have, and it's there."

Vernon Reid: The most important song on the record is the one that ends the record, but here's the thing, it's a song that you can write when things are going great, you know what I mean? The band is successful and you write this tune. And then this tune is still there during the divorce from my first wife. During the problem within Living Colour. It's there when the whole thing goes down. When the band takes its hiatus or breaks up. "This Is the Life" has been with me after my dreadlocks, and it's been with me through the ups and downs. It's been with me, and it's the kind of song you write in one space and because of what that song is saying, it is gonna be with you when the grand parade moves on. It's going to be with you. And it's interesting how people have connected to that song and it's also a song that we've all had to live with. When playing that song when everybody's not the best of friends on stage, and then when we realize that we love one another, it's there as well. It's there as our children are growing up. We're at that age where we're starting to lose parents, "This is the life you have," and it's there. It's there when you know, when Greg [Tate] first heard that song and now that Greg is gone, that song is there.

Dennis Diamond: When they did "This Is the Life," they recorded in total darkness. And it was actually the last song that they recorded in LA. The control room was darkened, and this was in the middle of the day. So, yeah, that was probably the more interesting thing that happened on that record that up until now nobody knew about. . . . We're a weird bunch of people. I don't think it was a conscious thing. I think they felt that it set a mood. . . . With "This Is the Life," they just felt it. They didn't need to see each other because they nailed it. There was a thing that we adhered to. We only play the song three times, and we take the best take of the three. They didn't edit parts of one song to the other. It was a complete performance, and that was important to them.

Greg Drew: I drove down to RPM and listened to what he'd [Corey] done. And you know how the beginning has that very sort of Middle Eastern kind of musical vibe? He was doing something similar to what is on the record, but because of the kind of singer that Corey was, it was much more sort of bluesy, sort of R&B/soul

kind of riffing. And you know, it's one of those things where it wasn't really wrong what he was doing. It just wasn't as good as it maybe could have been. So a day or two later, he and I talked about it, and I just said, "It doesn't sound quite right." And he said, "Well, what can we do?" And I said, "Well, maybe we should try doing some of the formal exercises that we did." And almost everything that we did was major scales and traditional Western vocal training. There isn't anything exotic about it. And I said, "Why don't I see if I can get somebody to teach me some different kinds of scales, and you could do the exercises with different kinds of scales. And that way, you'll be used to hearing different kinds of notes when you make your choices." And so, I think we talked to Ed and explained what we had in mind, and so for like a week, we did all the exercises that he'd been doing for a couple of years. It's just we did them with almost Raga-like scales. When we went back to redo the lead vocal, he did the main body of the song again, which he did better than he'd done it the previous time.

Corey Glover: Yeah, that's an amazing song. We [Glover and Drew] developed exercises around it, so that I could play within that mode. And again, it's not observational, it's experiential. What they say you are versus what you are. And I related to that completely. We're talking about finding your tribe, and them saying to you, you don't look like you'd be into this kind of thing. It's like, "Yeah, well, I am. In another life, I'd be you. But who I am is me."

Ed Stasium: It's so good. Lyrically, it's fantastic. "You'll always win the game/No one ever cheats you/You never have to change/Your friends never desert you." Beautiful. "Your loved ones never die, but this is the life you have." This is a sample [in the intro] that I think it was just a tambora sample of some sort there with Vernon riffing over it. Another insane soundscape. Insane. It's epic. What is it? We don't recognize that as any particular rock song, or sound, or guitar. What is it? Unbelievable. We have the backwards reverb on the lead vocal. . . . Corey turns into a different vocalist on this one. Who's that singing in the verses? He really goes into Corey in the choruses, but he puts on a character in the verses. It's a different personality. His acting is coming across there. What a great song. And it's a perfect ending.

Time's Up

"It's prophetic, yet at the same time it sounds as fresh as it did thirty years ago"

Ed Stasium: I can say that it's truly the only masterpiece that I ever worked on. I really find it to be a masterwork just because of the fluency from beginning to end, and how the songs intertwine. And it's cinematic. It's prophetic, yet at the same time it sounds as fresh as it did thirty years ago upon its release. But you know, unfortunately, the lyrical messages have not lost their relevance in those thirty years, which is kind of incredible.

Paul Hamingson: I never worked with bands where I didn't want to learn anything from them. And I learned a ton of stuff from Living Colour. Part of it about music and part of it about friendship and part of it about history and having a different perspective where that was not something that I necessarily had in my community, in my background, to understand that. I grew up in South Orange, which is on the border with Newark. I would have been nine, I think, when the '68 riots [Newark riots occurred in 1967] happened, and my parents took us out of town that summer. Maybe a couple years ago talking to my mom, she shared that my dad was scared at that point. It's hard to understand about how the music is woven through things when you don't understand how the history is woven through them.

Vernon Reid: I learned everything about producing from just checking out Ed Stasium and the way he thought about things and the way he utilized and captured small moments and the way he thought about music. And the thing also I loved about Ed and Paul was that whatever we were doing, and whatever we were talking about, they never flinched. We talked about very pointed things like "Someone Like You" and "History Lesson" and all the things we did. At no point did they ever pull me to the side. . . . "You know, that song 'Pride. . .'"

Greg Drew: I've had far less accomplished and successful producers than Ed [Stasium], who kind of viewed me as an enemy, or somebody that was gonna be in their way. And Ed was so much the opposite of that, that I'm eternally grateful to him.

Will Calhoun: So sound-wise, I just think Ed Stasium and Ron St. Germain are two of the best producers unsung in the world.

Ed Stasium: You know, I think my collaboration with Living Colour is kind of the pinnacle of what I consider to be a successful collaboration. It was a bonding. And that is so beautiful to me to be bonded with these guys for a lifetime.

Figure 1 Bassist Muzz Skillings. Photo courtesy of Paul Hamingson/Black Rock Coalition.

Figure 2 Engineer Paul Hamingson and producer Ed Stasium at the controls, with singer Corey Glover in the booth. Photo courtesy of Paul Hamingson/Black Rock Coalition.

Figure 3 Drummer Will Calhoun. Photo courtesy of Paul Hamingson/Black Rock Coalition.

Figure 4 Guitarist Vernon Reid and Will Calhoun after seeing Rush at the Great Western Forum. Photo courtesy of Paul Hamingson/Black Rock Coalition.

Figure 5 Guitar tech Dennis Diamond in the studio with Vernon Reid's guitars. Photo courtesy of Paul Hamingson/Black Rock Coalition.

3
"Pride"
Rock and Roll, Living Colour, and Me

It was a late Sunday afternoon in 1978 and I was nine. I sat in my Bed-Stuy, Brooklyn kitchen, watching the large, battered, stainless steel pot as it heated up on our equally-battered-and -now-yellowed-with-time stove. I eyed my grandmother, still dressed in her church clothes, while she stood watch nearby. She glanced at me, and I looked back. Uneasily. And then I quickly returned my focus to the blue flame that reached up and up, ever closer to the sides of the pot. I had never seen the burner set so high. "Kimberly, be careful with the burner. Keep it low," my mom would always tell me. My grandmother was humming to herself, which she often did, especially after church. I didn't recognize the song, but the words *lord* and *Jesus* stood out.

My mother was in our bedroom, having been chased there by my grandmother just minutes before. My mom had used the full weight of her five-foot-two-inch, 100-pound body to hold the door closed tight as my grandmother pulled and pulled using her own five-foot, and much heavier body. "You stupid bitch!" my mom taunted from behind the door.

"Get the fuck outta my house!" my grandmother shot back. Even though the words were familiar—my mom and I lived with my grandmother out of financial necessity and the two had some version of this same argument over and over again—they never lost their sting. I would flinch when my grandmother told my mom to leave because that included me too.

I looked away from the flame and saw my mom. She had come out of her room and was facing me. I held my breath. Why did I know what was coming while she did not? It didn't seem right. Before I could release my breath, my grandmother had pulled the pot off the stove and was hurling the boiling hot water at my mother. My mother was gone like a shot and the water barely connected, but I was terrified.

I grew up in a violent family. It was rage expressed in angry words and satiated in the completion of physical abuse. Grievances settled with a fist in a face or boiling water flung at a body. My mother and grandmother circled each other. Two women now both long gone, who were probably too much alike to have ever had the chance to coexist peacefully. My mother, having been physically and emotionally abused by her mother as a child and well into adulthood, was always braced for a fight, even as she did everything in her power to shy away from them. After divorcing my father when I was three, she stayed single until I was twelve to avoid getting hit. In her mind, all men hit eventually. When my mother shared the same space with my grandmother, even for fleeting minutes, all bets were off. These two equally broken and strong-willed women fought almost every time they crossed paths, which was daily.

I didn't know it then, but I internalized this violence and made myself small in order to make my mother's life easier. But I was also angry. When I said before that I grew up in a violent family, that was all true. But that doesn't tell the whole story. I also grew up in a musical family. My mother, grandmother, aunt, and uncles weren't professional musicians, but music was always there. My mother had a beautiful voice, and she sang all the time—around the house, to me, and later in the church choir when I was a teenager. As the story goes, when my mother was young, she was singing in a girl group that was good enough to have advanced far in a local talent show. In order to move forward to the next stage, she needed a nice dress and my grandmother was unsupportive, insisting that my mother couldn't "sing anyway."

Yet music was at the center of my grandmother's world, too. She sang along all day to a soundtrack that only she could hear. Sometimes she sang recognizable songs and other times she hummed melodies without words. I was always happy to hear my grandmother's singing. Not due to the singing itself, but because, usually, when she sang that meant that she had lost interest in whatever battle was occurring between her and my mom or she might be in too much of a good mood to fight. None of that was predictable though. Listening to music was also of value in our home, with my mother devouring rock music and influencing me to do the same. Rock offered a way for me to channel my quiet rage and Living Colour's *Time's Up* was the perfect sonic vehicle.

I grew up loving U2, Squeeze, and Blondie while enjoying Led Zeppelin, Cheap Trick, Van Halen, and other hard rock bands, but their music didn't quite hit the same way as Living Colour's. There are likely many reasons for this, but chief among them was that Living Colour rocked hard *and* they looked like me. Hearing "Time's Up," and the rest of *Time's Up*, in 1990 was one of the earliest moments where I felt joy in the aggression itself. Theirs and mine.

* * *

In addition to its aesthetic greatness, *Time's Up* has plenty to teach us. The second track is titled "History Lesson," and it instructs us that "in Africa, music is not an art form as much as it is a means of communication." The song after that, "Pride," a Will Calhoun contribution, grapples with the limits of the educational system in the United States, particularly around engaging histories and cultures of non-White people: "History's a lie that they teach you in school/A fraudulent view called the golden rule." This issue is still relevant today as we witness the moral panics around critical race theory— the great K–12 bogeyman. "Time's Up," the appropriately titled opening track of *Time's Up*, offers a wake-up call about the environmental crisis, specifically climate change: "The future won't save the past/The time is now ain't gonna last."

This wake-up call was urgent in 1990, and in the 2020s we face the profoundly sad reality that the battle may have already been lost. *Time's Up* sets out to put everyone on notice that it's imperative that these pressing social and political concerns be addressed. So many of these issues persist today—climate change, police brutality, and the shrinking middle class—which speaks to the timelessness of the record and the forward-thinking lyrical content of the band, with "Information Overload" effectively predicting the chaotic nature of the internet: "They say the future is on a microchip/Don't they know we're all on a sinking ship."

What else does this record teach us? Living Colour expand their palette on this album and instruct us on matters other than political and social issues. They educate us about the nature of love and the universal need to love and be loved and most importantly to love oneself. These ideas are explored in the songs "Love Rears Its Ugly Head," "Solace of You," and "This Is the Life." The ability of the band to tap into this universal need is something that Vernon Reid has thought about and it has become part of his and the band's ethos. As Reid shares:

[As a child] I'd hear Julie Andrews' "My Favorite Things" and just love the tune. That's the one thing I remember about the movie and that really connected to the first time I heard John Coltrane's version of "My Favorite Things." That was a kind of almost shock of recognition moment. Because I knew that John Coltrane fell in love with Julie Andrews' voice and those lyrics. And he based what he did off of his affection for that song. He wasn't playing it as a vehicle. Right? Oh, I'm just gonna blow over these changes. "When the dog bites/When the bee stings/When I'm feeling sad, I simply remember my favorite things, and then I don't feel so bad." And if you could put that in the context of being surrounded by trauma and the possibility of harm and fear, something like seizing on my favorite things, even as expressed by Julie Andrews, is a revolutionary act of healing. Seizing on the possibility of what that is, it's a radical act of humanness to find the common things that make us all human.

Sonically, *Time's Up* is a stunning album, with excellent songs, musicians at the top of their game, and great production. The soundscapes Living Colour created on this record feel current. The subject matter was particularly relevant in 1990, and of course it is still relevant today. But the sound alone holds up.

"Time's Up," "History Lesson," and "Pride" together set the tone for a record that is stylistically ambitious. While on the surface it appears that its greatest strength is its ability to engage multiple genres and forms, what Living Colour also does well on this record is demonstrate that these genres and forms are malleable, permeable, and in many cases fictional. As Reid states, "before the genres ossified and became rules you had to follow, there was a huge amount of freedom, and bands had their stance right. And did their thing." Skillings adds an important twist. Some critics who mentioned Living Colour's eclecticism used the term to undermine their legitimacy as rockers. But importantly, as Skillings notes, Living Colour's genre bending is not about the dilution of rock or seeking to create a fusion: "I was very conscious of the norms at the time and made very conscious, well-informed effort to expand the rock genre itself a bit at a time, while never violating the accepted rules of what rock was then. We pushed the boundaries by rocking through the boundaries." Skillings' "Ology" is certainly an example of this, as this short piece doesn't necessarily sound like rock. If one was interested in categorizing, it might be fair to suggest it's more like jazz—something more improvisational than rock, or at least normative hard rock—but all the tones and registers of the bass replicate all of the instruments a rock band normally plays, and the sounds are so moving that they evoke a passion that I feel when listening to rock. So why not include it in the rock genre? After all, music theorist Walter Everett evokes rock when discussing "Ology," calling it a "virtuosic, post-Hendrix six-bass jam."[1]

Time's Up is essential because it took a range of styles and genres of music (hardcore, hip-hop, funk, soul, and soukous) and pulled them together into an exciting rock mélange. It also allowed the band to rebel against expectations that the record would tread the same ground as *Vivid* or have obvious mainstream pop singles. And because of this, it's easy to see why producer Ed Stasium has drawn comparisons between *Time's Up* and the Beatles' cinematic *Sgt. Pepper's Lonely Hearts Club Band*, a record that never offered any singles: "This is basically a movie that you can listen to." It's in this spirit that the remainder of this chapter will consider, in vignettes, the sounds of Living Colour's *Time's Up* and how this work fits into my own story . . . .

*   *   *

I have no idea how many times I have listened to "Time's Up," but each time I do, I am struck by how powerful, exciting, heavy, moving, and immediate it remains. As soon as I hear the clocks and the insistent ticking that grows louder and louder, I find myself waiting, rapt, for the Snap! Snap! Snap! of Calhoun's drums. He hits those drums like he's mad at them—and I get it. The band has always talked about their love and admiration for the Bad Brains and "Time's Up" is a clear homage. It was also the fulfillment of Glover's long-time love for hardcore and desire to sing a hardcore or punk rock song. And "Time's Up" certainly fits the bill. It has the blinding speed and sledgehammer aggression of the Bad Brains' "Sailin On" and "Don't Need It," and the ingenious changes and unexpected melody of "Banned in D.C." I always appreciate the changes in this song. The move from the furious hardcore with Skillings' simultaneously rhythmic and melodic, muscular, and delicate bass line and Calhoun's lightning-fast drumming to a slowed-down funkier hard rock song is unexpected but feels right every time.

Real talk. I didn't grow up in an Afrocentric home. I want to be clear that I was reared in a family of proud Black people, including numerous Black women who modeled independence for me. And during the 1970s, when I was seven or eight, my mother gifted me with the *Black Book*, a chronicle of Black American history from 1619 to the 1940s. But my mother did not allow me to watch *Roots* on TV because she was certain that it would scare me and inform my worldview. In other words, she was concerned that I would grow up to be afraid of White people, which certainly didn't align with her plans for my successful assimilation into mainstream White culture. I might go so far as to label my mother a feminist but given that many of the feminists she admired were White women—*Our Bodies, Ourselves* was a staple in our home—it is fair to say that it was not an intersectional brand of feminism. And all of this converges with the other message I didn't get growing up—that rock is Black. My mother and I were passionate fans of rock, but I was never explicitly told where the music came from. She played Jimi Hendrix, Thin Lizzy, and Garland Jeffreys in our home, but mostly without political comment.

So in 1990, my engagement (or lack thereof) with the next two songs is reflective of these aspects of my upbringing. When I first heard "History Lesson," and for years afterward, with its invocation of Africa, I would fast-forward (this was in the days of cassette tapes) to get to the part that rocks. Of course, thirty-two years later, my education—formal and informal—in Black American history has reshaped my interests and views, but my history behind "History Lesson" is important as it shows why Living Colour has made such an impact on me and my musical development.

On Will Calhoun's song "Pride," Reid's guitar riff is BIG. On an album featuring propulsive guitar on multiple hard rock songs, this riff is particularly memorable. The drums are heavy, and Glover's voice is thunderous, while Skillings' bass line is unobstructive and mellifluous. "Don't ask me why I play this music/'Cause it's my culture, so naturally I use it/I state my claim to say, it's here for all to play." These lyrics struck a chord from the moment I first heard it. I was unsure of myself. I thought rock was White. Living Colour gave me permission to love this music and to embrace it as my own.

* * *

Like many other rock-loving little girls in 1979—at the height of Blondie's commercial success—Debbie Harry was my hero and like most everyone else in that time period, I was in awe of her beauty. I loved Blondie's music, but I also spent a lot of time staring at Debbie's face on album covers, and in rock magazines and glossy color books. I wondered how someone could have such perfect cheekbones and pouty full lips, while also seeming like she didn't care one bit about her face or her body. How could someone look like a classic Hollywood movie star, while onstage contorting her body awkwardly as she danced with wild abandon? Her physical beauty attracted me but also repelled me because the elements of her face that made her an object of admiration and lust were elements that would, as a young Black girl, elude me. My hair was not straight. My skin was not porcelain white. My face was not simultaneously angular and soft, with just the right accentuation of the cheekbone. Debbie's beauty reminded me of what I was not. This did not inhibit my passionate and abiding fandom for her and her band, but it kept me at a distance in much the same way I negotiated the gulf between the White male rock stars I crushed on and myself.

When I sat on my living room couch, "Oh Caroline" by Cheap Trick on the turntable, I fantasized that *I* was Caroline and Robin Zander was talking to me: "Oh Caroline, my life shined when you walked in." But I had already gotten the message that that would only be possible if I were a White girl. So when I closed my eyes, pretending to be Caroline, I would still be me, only I would flip my hair—my cornrowed braids—the way the White girls on TV and at my prep school in Brooklyn Heights did. I never questioned any of this. Growing up in 1970s Brooklyn, rock stars were White. The women they celebrated and derided, in equal measure, were White. And rock music itself was White. The music I loved the most was not for me. Sure, I was free to listen to it, but I was constantly reminded when I read *Creem* and *Rolling*

Stone and, later when I started going to rock shows, that I was an interloper.

On a cold evening in February 1981, I attended my first rock show with my mom: Cheap Trick at Radio City Music Hall in Manhattan. I was eleven. My mom used a ticket broker to score center floor seats about fifteen rows back. Cheap Trick was one of my favorite bands. Second only to Blondie, I was obsessed with the four men from Rockford, Illinois—I played both *Cheap Trick at Budokan* and *Dream Police* nonstop at home. I knew that they were an acclaimed live band—one of those bands who spent many of their pre-fame years on the road honing their touring chops in small clubs—because *Rolling Stone* magazine had told me so. They did not disappoint. Singer Robin Zander, known as the man of a thousand voices, thrilled the crowd with his alternatively soft crooning and always-in-tune, aggressive screaming, and guitarist Rick Nielson showcased his impressive range of now-iconic heavy rock riffs.

As it was my first concert, I spent as much time looking around at the audience as I did focusing on the spectacle on stage. I immediately noticed that I didn't see another Black face besides mine and my mom's. And it was not for lack of trying. I searched and searched. It didn't take long for the discomfort and self-consciousness to kick in.

As the concert continued, I was sure that people were staring at us. I became distracted, lost in thought, as the band I had been dreaming about seeing live for so long stood before me. I loved the music more than anything, but I wasn't sure if I was supposed to be there. I wasn't sure if the music was *for* me. A little more than halfway through the show, Cheap

Trick played their cover of Fats Domino's rock and roll classic "Ain't That a Shame." I knew Fats Domino was Black, and I figured most of the audience did too. This was a tiny opening that helped me feel a little bit less like an outsider. Hearing that song made me happy. But the feeling was fleeting.

As much as I enjoyed my first rock show, it was the second one that helped me to fall in love with live rock performance. On a hot, sticky July evening in 1981—July 17, 1981, to be exact—I saw Van Halen at Madison Square Garden. I had turned twelve a month earlier. I stood next to my mom, wide eyed, peering down at the band from the balcony stage left, as absolute rock and roll chaos unfolded in front of us. Van Halen began their set, as they often did in their early shows, with "On Fire" from their self-titled debut. This underrated hard rock classic features a catchy (and, of course, heavy) guitar riff by the late Eddie Van Halen and the highest of high falsetto vocals by singer David Lee Roth and bassist Michael Anthony in the chorus. All night, Roth prowled the stage, the embodiment of rock and roll swagger, in impossibly tight gray satin pants and a ripped white T-shirt. That is when he wasn't shirtless.

There was an endless parade of solos: bass solos, drum solos, and, of course, Eddie was Eddie, a god with the guitar, to the delight of the rhapsodic crowd. At one point during the show, Roth, ever the showman, emerged from backstage with his oversized blue ice cream bar guitar for his cover of Chicago bluesman John Brim's song "Ice Cream Man." That image is forever seared into my brain. But once again, as I looked at the audience to my left and my right, and across the arena, I saw a sea of Whiteness. The only Black people

I witnessed were staff members working as ushers and manning the concession stands. So I continued to believe that rock was White. I loved it, and my mom did too. It spoke to me like no other music could, but when I played my records at home, I was always worried our neighbors might hear. And I feared they would judge me.

I know now, what I did not know then: Rock is Black. Evolving out of the blues and, later, rhythm and blues, rock and roll *c.* 1950s to early1960s, had a Black face, with artists like Chuck Berry and Little Richard and Fats Domino and Big Joe Turner leading the way. Yet, as rock and roll gave way to rock, it became associated with Whiteness, with Elvis, the British Invasion acts, and later Led Zeppelin, appropriating and regurgitating Black American music back to young White fans. At that time, I had certainly heard of Jimi Hendrix. My mom wouldn't stop talking about him. But he had been gone for more than a decade. I was a one-year-old when he died. My mother also told me stories about Black singer-songwriter Arthur Lee, and his Los Angeles-based rock band Love, who never enjoyed the success that they deserved. Phil Lynott was also Black and alive and important. He was the front man for Thin Lizzy, an internationally successful, hard rockin' crew from Dublin, Ireland. But Dublin, particularly in 1978 when my mom would play "Dancing in the Moonlight" on the living room stereo, might as well have been on the moon. Even if these Black artists demonstrated that rock music wasn't the exclusive purview of White men, where were the Black fans when I went to concerts?

* * *

I was in love when I first heard "Love Rears Its Ugly Head." I thought the song was funny (particularly the melodramatic soap opera score opening), but I also related to the song deeply. Not because I had any sort of fear of commitment or had any desire whatsoever to get married to anyone at that time but because I understood for the first time that true love involves trust and communication and when you trust someone you don't worry if they don't come home early or call. In other words, you learn to love with a loose grip. And it was my favorite song to sing alongside Glover who gives a terrific vocal performance. Glover told me that he decided to deliver the vocals as a blues singer rather than an R&B or rock singer. And given that the great blues singers are storytellers all, Glover made a great artistic choice. Though the music does not confirm to a blues form or sound like a blues and is instead reminiscent of a jazzy R&B song, Reid's guitar keeps the song firmly in the rock idiom. His solo and the guitar break after the bridge "rock," though the short break also evokes the blues. These genre wanderings once again demonstrate how Living Colour crosses musical boundaries as an act of expansion. No matter how bluesy Glover's vocal delivery is, "Love Rears Its Ugly Head" is a rock song.

The storytelling perspective in "New Jack Theme"—the first-person account of an unapologetic, successful drug dealer—was always striking to me, and the music, with its beats and synths, creates a house music, party vibe. And this sonic treatment makes great sense. After all, the character in the song is celebratory: "I make more money than a judge or a cop/Give me a reason why I should stop." The break in the middle invites the listener into the party and insists that they dance. But this section is complex and jarring, with its dance beats and Reid's metal guitar solo, much like the protagonist's existence. I'm not suggesting the drug dealer narrator is conflicted about his choices because he is not. But the listener is left to make sense of their own feelings. The drug dealer is endangering his own community, yet it is also difficult to answer his question. Given his life circumstances, why should he stop?

I sometimes marvel at how I came of age during the Reagan 1980s and at a time when White was the default in every realm of American culture. If I wanted to see Black people on television, I had to watch a "Black show" on a "Black channel." While I would not say that it was any more racist then than it is now, there are so many things that occurred as I was growing up that I never questioned and few around me did either. Not only were microaggressions unnamed, unacknowledged, and unabating, but Black folks were expected to just roll with them, bottling up their anger for later. I also knew how dangerous it was for Black men and women in NYC, and across the country, but somehow, I remained unscathed, at least physically. "Someone Like You" always takes me back to an uncertain time when I was young, innocent, very much in peril, and living in a NYC that no longer exists. A Manhattan with rents that were more expensive than most of the rest of the United States, yet I could live below 42nd street with a roommate (both of us young Black women without generational wealth) for $800.00/month during my senior year of college. At the same time, as Trey Ellis reminded us, the 1980s/early 1990s was a terrible time for Black people in the United States. The children's voices at the beginning of the song certainly reflect this. The voices are happy, excited, *innocent* at first, and then the soundscape slowly turns into a waking nightmare with the peaceful sounds morphing into what can only be described as a sonic "scream."

"Yo, Corey Man." "Yeah Man, What's Up?" "I saw Elvis the other day." "Get outta here, Man!" "Elvis Is Dead" always makes me smile. The James Brown-esque break. The Little Richard and Maceo Parker cameos. The glee with which Living Colour pokes fun at the Elvis mythology. And this song appeared right around the time that Richard Penniman was everywhere, making appearances at award shows and participating in his own narrative self-reinvention. He *was* an architect of rock and roll, and he wasn't afraid to let everyone know it. And how perfect that he joined forces with a band whose mission was, in part, to reclaim the Black origins of rock.

Reid's driving guitar riff in "Type" is everything. But Glover's vocal performance gets me every time—"Everything that goes around comes around"—alongside Reid's lightning-fast playing and Skillings' background vocals. I would sing this along with Glover in my living room and it was tough! The breath control on this song is impressive. This is a song that provides a great example of how a vocal coach can help a singer.

Of course, Reid's guitar sounds like a computer on "Information Overload." What we think of when we think of space-age fantasy narratives, with plenty of bleeps and bloops and a hypnotic riff and a compelling groove. There are so many changes. "I don't want to live like this." It feels like four different songs. Even the breakdown sounds like a doomsday soundtrack. Listening to this song in 1990 felt like I was engaging the realm of science fiction. I needed to fear our "future on a microchip," like I needed to be concerned with driving a flying car Jetsons-style. Hearing it now, I shake my head wondering how Reid wrote this song before the widespread public use of email.

Coming of age during the early part of the HIV and AIDS epidemic made "Under Cover of Darkness" an obvious song I could relate to. I was aware of the statistics at that time— straight Black women were the most vulnerable population besides gay men. So I was *very* nervous about contracting HIV. It was safe sex or no sex for me. But in 1990, I wanted my rock hard, so I often skipped over this song. Now when I listen to it, I'm impressed with the band's willingness to include a song promoting safe sex, while presenting a woman's perspective on the issue. And the music—especially Glover's vocal performance and Latifa's flow—offered a cool and sophisticated sexiness. So Glover's desire to "make a song about safe sex sexy" succeeded.

"Ology" is a wonderful example of Skillings' "rocking through the boundaries." In this all-bass (besides a drum loop) jazzy offering, Skillings layers multiple bass sounds. Beginning with bass lines of varying lengths and tones and culminating with a beautiful solo that acts as the perfect segue to "Fight the Fight," demonstrating Skillings' uniqueness as a player.

Reid's guitar intro to "Fight the Fight" flows perfectly from Skillings' solo. And Calhoun's drums are so funky. James Brown-level funky. He can play anything. He can pound the crap out of the drums with a powerful rock or metal sound, give you jazzy fills, or lay on the funk.

"Tag Team Partners" always feels so New York and so joyful. I can feel the warmth between Doug E. Fresh and Glover—those two were friends before Glover joined Living Colour. This close relationship is reflected in the easy give and take between the two men. The call and response they have using their voices. And as a fan of old school hip-hop then and now, I appreciated the beatboxing.

"Solace of You" is a beautiful song. It's an example of the ways in which the band crosses genre boundaries (soukous!) or, as Skillings suggested to me, expands the rock idiom. The vocals (lead and background) are stunning. In my rockist early twenties, I would fast-forward past this song too. But now that I know the devastation of losing a parent—in this case, my mom—I have a profound appreciation for Glover's lyrics: "Gotta go inside back where it started/Back to the beginning 'cause that's where my heart is." In many ways my heart is arrested. When my mother died in 2015, I had a brief moment of wondering how I could go on. But go on I did. And the rawest, most tender part of the pain has acquired a layer of protection that helps me to see all that I do have and that she's also always with me.

"In your real life, treat it like it's special/In your real life, try to be more kind/In your real life, think of those that love you/In this real life, try to be less blind." At twenty-one, "This Is the Life" changed the way I lived or at least the way I hoped to live. This song, which begins as a quiet, psychedelic invocation and ends as a swelling rock anthem, offered an aspirational version of my life. This is one of the few songs

I can think of where the message remains as personally resonant today as it was thirty-two years ago.

At nine, I knew I wanted to be a writer. I went to college at NYU where I majored in playwriting and screenwriting. I grew up loving musical theater and I was lucky to have a mom who cultivated that interest, taking me to Broadway shows and children's theater throughout New York City. As I listened to "This Is the Life" on my boom box in my bedroom in my first real apartment, a sixth-floor walkup in Kips Bay that I shared with my friend Aleeka, I worried that I would never be successful. I worried that all my dreams would remain just that. *Dreams.*

It was my senior year, and I was writing a screenplay for my senior capstone. It was about a Black woman jazz singer in the first half of the twentieth century and the clandestine relationship she has with a White male doctor from a wealthy family. I was young, so I thought I might be able to sell it to a Hollywood studio, but there was a part of me that knew that was unlikely to happen. At a freshman mentor breakfast three years earlier, I had already been told as much by a White male faculty member, who had also written the screenplay for an Academy Award–nominated film. He wasn't only talking to me. He told a group of young women of various races that none of us had a chance in Hollywood. That the doors were simply closed to us. At eighteen, his words shook my confidence and negatively affected my experience in the program. This same professor, after reading my screenplay in 1991 at the end of my senior year, called me at home to tell me how much he loved my work. He also apologized, but it was too late.

But that conversation hadn't happened yet, and as I listened to Glover's voice encouraging me to appreciate what I *do* have, I felt better. I have gone back to that song many times over the years, as I continued my arduous path toward becoming a writer, becoming a parent, and learning to be someone who can see the value in having gratitude for all the good in my life. I still don't always treat my "real life" like "it's special," but I'm working on it.

4
"Information Overload"
The Critics Weigh In

They are not just saying words to be saying them. I think black people need to support them as well as white people, to realize the contribution that they are making at this time. The same thing that started in the Fifties with me, they are taking it through the Nineties. And God bless their souls. They are keeping it alive.
—Little Richard, *Rolling Stone*, November 1, 1990[1]

Not since Led Zeppelin has a hard-rock band sounded so recklessly commanding, so eager to push every song to its outer limits. Like Zeppelin, Living Colour pumps every style of music imaginable through its massive stacks of amplifiers, from hip-hop to jazz, and emerges with something new.
—Greg Kot, *Chicago Tribune*, November 8, 1990[2]

What does it mean when a fan or a critic declares an artist, a band, or a specific musical work to be underrated or underappreciated? How do we measure such a thing? The answer to this is not as straightforward as it may seem. Sometimes artists or bands enjoy regional or local successes and perhaps even influence other musicians but never enjoy (or seek) mainstream, national success. And sometimes artists or bands sell lots of albums, but critics and other taste-making apparatuses (award-granting organizations, for example) remain skeptical, so there's room for fans, and perhaps a small minority of critics, to decide that the band is underrated, or a particular work has been overlooked. And then there are bands such as Living Colour whose greatness was noted in real time by fans and critics alike. Their first album *Vivid*—with its song "Cult of Personality" winning a Grammy, one of the most prestigious awards a musical artist or band can win—was a commercial and critical success. Their second album, *Time's Up*, was even more critically acclaimed than their first, with many critics seeing a creative evolution in the band's music. It also sold well and moved up the charts quickly, faster than *Vivid* had in the United States: "According to Living Colour co-manager Jim Grant, Epic initially shipped 400,000 copies of the album; before the week was out, the reorders were coming in. What's more, rock radio—which was last to get on the bandwagon for *Vivid*—embraced the leadoff single, 'Type,' right out of the box. The track went to the Top Ten in AOR airplay."[3] But then sales slowed down. Even so, they won a second consecutive Grammy award for *Time's Up*. They were nominated for two other Grammys, including one for "Leave it Alone" from their 1993 album *Stain*. In 1989, they won three MTV Music Awards for "Cult of Personality" and "Newcomer of the Year" at the International Rock Awards.

Yet for some critics and fans, Living Colour remain an underrated or underappreciated band, with *Time's Up* being particularly so.[4,5]

I, too, have put Living Colour in the underrated category even though they have enjoyed the kinds of successes that, statistically, few aspiring bands will ever experience—achieving popularity, favorable reviews, and other accolades right out of the gate. They are still the most commercially successful all-Black rock band since 1970's *Band of Gypsies* went double platinum.[6] But now I realize that it's not that Living Colour didn't get their due. It's that Living Colour's major commercial success did not sustain itself long enough for their work to be deeply engaged by a larger public over a long period of time. This matters because in a culture that encourages and facilitates instant gratification, if an artist or a band is not trending on the prominent social media platforms or appearing on popular news sites, they might as well not exist. So while Living Colour's work was lauded in the late 1980s/early 1990s, the full scope and depth of their legacy have been obscured. Of course, the diehard fans who were there from the beginning remember their enormous impact when they first emerged and recognize that they have more than fulfilled their early promise as the decades have passed. But the fans who jumped on the bandwagon when they heard "Cult of Personality" and jumped off before *Time's Up* have not been charting their career and likely do not remember how exceptional they were and still are. But the critics always knew. Even as they spent a disproportionate amount of time focusing on the complexions of the men in Living Colour, they also always lauded the band's musical talent and uniqueness. What follows is a compilation of reviews of *Time's Up* and the supporting North American tour. These reviews are from a wide range of publications—some dedicated to music like *Rolling Stone* and more general newspapers with sections focused on the arts. I begin with a quick note on the tonal shift from *Vivid*-era press coverage to *Time's Up*.

*　*　*

Living Colour's *Vivid*-era press engaged the band on two registers: a band and a movement. The press was mostly behind the movement, with writers grappling with how rock became coded as White despite its indisputably Black origins. The movement seemed like it could encroach on the music if everyone was not careful. The music was hard to ignore given its quality. Still, virtually all the stories, and their headlines, focused on Living Colour's race and their decision to play rock music. And there were plenty of problematic articles and writers on both sides of the Atlantic who were condescending even as they attempted to compliment the band.

In a 1989 article in the *Shreveport Times*, Tom Turco declares, "Living Colour is as much a state of mind, as it is a rock 'n' roll band. The black quartet's very existence challenges racial attitudes while its music defies casual stereotyping, sounding almost like 'Smokey Robinson meets Eddie Van Halen.'"[7] While this opening is meant to highlight the band's political *and* musical importance, rather than modeling how to defy "casual stereotyping,"

Turco participates in it himself. Why not compare Living Colour to Van Halen and leave it at that? Why not engage Living Colour as a rock band with a capacious view of the genre rather than suggesting a fusion? As Muzz Skillings said to me about *Time's Up*, though it is also relevant here, "Very often comments about *Time's Up* being eclectic were coming from an intention of subjecting us to othering. Code phrases like a soulful vocal performance, or funk rock, funky rock, etc., as opposed to calling a particular expression rock, that was an attempt to just kind of 'other' us."

In a 1988 live review in England's *Melody Maker*, Ian Gittins shares that he arrives at the show with: "Doubts about the clumsy manifesto tucked under their arms, about funk-metal fusion, about how black men can rock. Even the name seems too overt. Are they just up there with a point to prove? Is it worth it?" The answer, it turns out, is a resounding yes: "Doubts shrivel when they hit top gear." And in the end, Gittins suggests that we should "Forget the altruistic motivations we all foisted on them. They just want to be loud and joyous and bark at the moon."[8] But the damage is already done. The writer, in print, admits that he had doubts that Black people can play a genre of music that they invented. This rhetorical approach of questioning Living Colour's rock legitimacy—and then saying, in effect, "Never mind, they rock after all!"—has a similar otherizing effect.

Finally, in a 1989 *Melody Maker* article by Paul Lester, Anthrax's manager, erupts in anger when he is asked why the band chose Living Colour as an opening act for their European tour:

Do you mind if I just add a comment here, for what it's worth? Do you know the most racist bunch of f***in' people? The f***in' press! Anthrax take a band on tour, f***in' period, and cos they're black there are more f***in' questions. . . . You guys are making a f***in' issue out of this! This is a great band *(meaning Living Colour)* and a great big period! Everyone is saying, "It's a bold move Anthrax did." F***in' bold! It's a show!⁹

*   *   *

In 1990, when *Time's Up* released, some of the Black-rock-band novelty had worn off, so critics began to focus a bit more on the music than the movement. That is not to say that the question of race and genre disappeared. Those questions and conversations endured, but the press spent more time on the music itself. The reviews of *Time's Up* were almost universally stellar, whether they were in major music publications such as *Rolling Stone*; national newspapers like the *New York Times*; regional alternative weeklies like the *L.A. Weekly*; or smaller regional newspapers and collegiate publications, such as Utah's Weber State University's *The Signpost*. In some cases, in their reviews, writers lamented that major labels had not already lined up to sign a wave of Black rockers after Living Colour's spectacular success. As George Varga at Utah's *The Spectrum* notes, "while record companies usually rush out to sign as many clones of U2, Def Leppard or whatever band is rock's current flavor of the month, there has been a conspicuous lack of black rock band signings in the wake of Living Colour's success with 'Vivid,' and its even more adventurous successor, 'Time's Up.'"[10] Greg Tate also reflected on this in our July 2021 interview:

> But Living Colour cracked the top 40. They cracked MTV. They were in that conversation in a way that the Brains and Fishbone never got to be because you gotta have that one record in that period, that just becomes a top-40 record. And then you go to the Grammys and the MTV awards. Part of their success and contribution was breaking it on those multiple platforms. There was no other Black band comparable. And really you kind of realize that it's also the Highlander thing. There can only be one. So after them it had to be Rage Against the Machine and after Rage it was TV on the Radio and since then who? Nobody.

While Black Rock Coalition (BRC) bands Eye & I and Total Eclipse were signed to major labels after Living Colour's success—Epic and A&M respectively, with both albums releasing in 1992—BRC members believed that the bands did not receive the marketing and promotional support they needed to succeed commercially.[11] Black rock bands that influenced, or were contemporaries of Living Colour, such as the Bad Brains and BRC band 24-7 SPYZ, were also signed to major labels for the first time in the early 1990s. With Living Colour's assistance, Epic released the Bad Brains' 1993 album *Rise*.[12] EastWest/Atlantic Records released the 24-7 SPYZ' EP *This Is . . . 24-7 SPYZ* in 1991 and their full-length album *Strength in Numbers* was released in 1992.[13] And Fishbone, who had been signed to Columbia Records since the 1980s, enjoyed their greatest commercial success with their third album, 1991's *The Reality of My Surroundings*, which reached #49 on the US Billboard 200 Chart.[14]

In November 1990, Living Colour was featured on the cover of *Rolling Stone*, with David Fricke offering this praise, "Musically, Living Colour's refusal to simply fall back on the funk-metal meal ticket of *Vivid* illustrates the band members' deep-rooted spiritual resolve."[15] And in a story for the *Los Angeles Times*, Steve Hochman shares the following exchange he had with the band:

> The four members of Living Colour responded to the first question in unison and so emphatically it sounded rehearsed.
>
> The question was, "Should anyone still care that you're a *black* hard-rock band?"
>
> The answer: "No!"
>
> For all intents, the response *was* rehearsed. The issue of race has been with Living Colour since it began in the mid-'80s, and the band would like nothing more than to lose it. After all, Living Colour established itself on grounds that have nothing to do with race.[16]

It is important to note that even when it may have seemed that the band was forced to talk about race when they might not feel like it, the intelligence and clarity that they brought to these conversations were crucial. It was necessary that they shed light on historic and contemporary erasures of Black people from rock. That they highlighted how terrible the 1980s were for Black people, despite their own success. That they celebrated their difference and their simultaneous universal humanity. But these conversations, in that time and place, always threatened to overshadow the music. *Time's Up* is too good for that to have happened completely, but in terms of continued mainstream success they became a message band and some fans probably lost interest in that. And as the music became more experimental, more challenging than the best of hard rock—more complex than Van Halen or Led Zeppelin—it gave casual fans of the band a reason to move on. Even so, as much as Living Colour may have been tired of talking about race, it was (and is) a crucial part of their life's work.

The rave reviews of *Time's Up* continued to pour in from publications throughout North America and the UK. In the *Montreal Gazette's* Rock Talk column, Mark Lepage states, "If you're Living Colour, you buckle down, remember where you came from, and deliver a record whose aggressiveness, risk-taking, and uncompromising lyrics are its greatest strength."[17] In the *Burlington Free Press's* Nightlife column, Scott Sutherland asserts, "'Time's Up' proves, beyond any doubt, that these guys are hard-hitting rockers and are here to stay."[18] The *New York Times'* Jon Pareles asserts, "With the best intentions, the songs work to be catchy as well as righteous," and adds that "sometimes bands grow more didactic as they grow more popular; Living Colour knows better, and *Time's Up* pulverizes anything that threatens to confine the music."[19] In the *Lincoln Journal Star*, L. Kent Wolgamott states:

Taking on all the standard hard rock elements and recasting them with bits of funk and even a couple of references to rap and jazz, Living Colour makes crunching guitar vital again and Glover's vocals are those of a singer reaching his peak. Those elements in combination make "Time's Up" not only one of the year's most important records, but one of its most listenable. Living Colour has found hard rock's future, so listen up.[20]

And finally, in a review in Q, Charles Shaar Murray describes Time's Up as:

avant-metal rock with as high a crunch-factor as anything else you can find in a record store these days, with Reid's squibbling, firebreathing guitar continually butting heads against Skilling's [sic] slam-dunk bass around Calhoun's muscle-packed drumming and Glover's much-improved singing. Nevertheless, their pointed lyrics and major musical smarts deserve to get Living Colour heard a long way beyond headbanging territory. And can they rock? Does Saddam Hussein like invading small countries?[21]

After Time's Up was released, Living Colour went back on the road. The tour with the Rolling Stones long over, they were the headliners playing theaters, colleges, and multi-night stands in some of the clubs that a few years earlier offered much more modest audience turnout. The Time's Up tour began in North America on November 2, 1990, in upstate New York at SUNY New Paltz. They played multiple nights in cities like Chicago and their hometown of New York City.[22] While reviews of the album were positive, the write-ups about the first leg of the North American tour were mixed. This is surprising given how Living Colour has always been a strong live band. Some of these negative, or mixed, reviews were born of a good-faith engagement with the music, while it appeared that others came from folks who were perhaps already predisposed to dislike the band's music in the first place.

On December 11 and 12, 1990, Living Colour played two shows at the Academy in New York City, the site of my first Living Colour concert. Writers from the *New York Daily News*, the *New York Times*, and *Newsday* reviewed the opening night. Two of the reviews were negative, but most surprising was the dismissive tone of one of the writers: In a review in *Newsday* John Leland shared that he enjoyed Maceo Parker's saxophone solo during "Elvis Is Dead," and a few other songs, most notably Living Colour's cover of "Amazing Grace," but he thought outside of those moments the band seemed to be competing onstage, fighting for individual musical supremacy rather than working to fit together. He then takes the time to mention a shift that occurred between the success *of Vivid*, during which Living Colour attracted a new and different audience, and post-*Vivid* as they toured a new record:

The show was a homecoming date, but an uncertain one. "Time's Up" dropped unceremoniously out of Billboard magazine's Top 100 this week, after a fairly short stay of 13 weeks. Scalpers on 43rd Street were asking $10 for $20 tickets. The headbangers and metal youth, who made last year's homecoming at the Ritz, a rough-and-tumble boyfest stayed away for the most part, as did the masses of black bohemians. Instead, the hall filled up with the collegiate, alternative music audience that first supported the band.[23]

In a review for the *New York Times*, jazz guitarist and former music critic, Peter Watrous, discussed how he was unimpressed with Skillings' and Will Calhoun's ability to keep a rhythm going, while also suggesting that Living Colour's material itself is subpar: "It's not a good sign when a band's best songs are covers of somebody else's old songs, and when the most musical moments of a show come from a guest." And later, "Song after song, many taken from the group's newest album, 'Time's Up,' blurred under the frustrating inability of the rhythm section to play cleanly." And further expressing his exasperation with the rhythm section, "Sticking to banal rhythmic ideas reinforced the one-dimensionality of the performance. The band can often overcome its material and has given more than its share of exceptional shows, but on Tuesday night the material won."[24] This review particularly rankled Reid. As he told Mark Prado in *Living Colour: Beyond the Cult of Personality*:

> What was crazy about it was that we played those nights and we killed. Maybe our reach exceeded our grasp. But I thought of that period of the band, those are some of our best shows. We dance on the line between real improvisation and total self-indulgence. It's dangerous. We are a band that takes risks both good and ill. We have been celebrated for it and we have been put down for it.[25]

The take by the *New York Daily News'* Michael Saunders was more mixed, with his seeing the merit in the new music, while also pointing out the moments of "sloppy" playing that in his estimation are an important component of rock and roll: "Tuesday's show at the Academy on W. 43rd St., was a streamlined attack on rock's complacent side and a denial of the dreaded sophomore slump that some critics expected before the fall release of their second album, 'Time's Up.'" He adds:

> What didn't work? Glover and Reid both droned on at times, letting flashy solos go past the point of appreciation. A few songs suffered from sloppy midsections, when the energy level romped out of control and bassist Muzz Skillings and drummer Will Calhoun momentarily missed connections. But such miscues are the sign of hard driving rock bands that take chances. Living Colour fits that bill.[26]

And finally, Greg Kot at the *Chicago Tribune*, with some caveats, offered a strong review of one of the shows on Living Colour's sold out, three-night stand at the Cabaret Metro in Chicago. "It's not always an easy listen. The brilliant current single, 'Type,' sounded rushed, the song's momentous finale a blur instead of a tidal wave. Other songs occasionally seemed to collapse instead of end decisively. And technical difficulties bogged down 'Pride' in midsong." He continues, "But it's the mistakes, the oddly bent notes, the sheer abandon, that make Living Colour such an exciting band. Vernon Reid's guitar solos seemed to start in mid-sentence and explode in a dozen directions before resolving."[27] While critics like Saunders and Kot see the rock and roll in the chaos, it appears that other critics missed the point. The review by Watrous, in particular, makes me wonder if the other critics who prefer Skillings and Calhoun "play cleanly" understand the scene that Living Colour came out of, and their appreciation for bands like the Bad Brains. This unpredictability and looseness give the band their energy and excitement. And I wonder too if because all four members of Living Colour are exceptional music makers, and, most importantly, technically proficient on their instruments (including voice), were they being held to a higher standard than your average rock band? Even if an undercurrent of their work, especially live, embraces a punk rock ethos, they perhaps were penalized when they let the music take them where *it* wanted to go versus orchestrating every moment. I also sense some defensiveness on the part of the critics who did not engage Living Colour's live shows in good faith. Reviews that focused as much on Living Colour's commercial decline as their music, for example, afforded power to the critic as they quietly protected the status quo: rock music played exclusively by White people.

Prior to writing this book, I was sure I would find negative reviews for *Time's Up*. But that did not happen. Aside from the mixed reception for some of their live shows (there were also plenty of positive ones), the critical feedback for the *Time's Up* album was consistently positive. Living Colour was never underrated. The question of legacy, however, remains.

5
"This Is the Life"
Aftermath and Legacy

At first, it appeared that *Time's Up* might be as commercially successful as *Vivid*. *Time's Up* went gold quickly, selling over 500,000 copies in a month. This contrasted with the rhythm of *Vivid*'s success. It took some time for *Vivid* to gain traction—opening for the Rolling Stones helped Living Colour find their audience. By the time they released and toured behind *Time's Up*, they had an eager fan base that was excited to see where the band would take them next. Living Colour would win their second consecutive Grammy for *Time's Up* in 1991.[1,2] But album sales for *Time's Up* stalled.

Time's Up was a very different album. It offered more sonic and lyrical complexity and diversity than *Vivid*, and from the perspective of Vernon Reid, it was "Blacker than anything Living Colour has done." As Reid explains, "we really start thinking about a larger, longer time scale and also bigger questions. They were more like a song like 'Time's Up.' So I was thinking it would be great to do something that's almost like a tribute to the Bad Brains, because Bad Brains out of D.C. have redefined hardcore and punk in a big way." Other songs on the record speak to questions and investments of Black Americans such as "Information Overload," which, with its focus on technology run amok, considers a potential Black future, evoking Afrofuturism. And, of course, "History Lesson" and "Pride" talk directly to Black listeners about how they are perceived in the United States. Corey Glover also sees an evolution from *Vivid* to *Time's Up* that suggests a movement toward interrogating subjects that are even more focused on lived experiences. In other words, *Time's Up* is the sound of a band embracing the ways in which they are uniquely qualified to engage and report back on matters of keen interest to Black Americans. As Glover put it: "We have a perspective that's very unique. We're not tied to the past. We're not trying to reinvent something. But there are things that we understand about the world we live in. It's not just 'Cult of Personality.' 'Cult of Personality' said a lot, but so did a song like 'Pride.'"

And Muzz Skillings also spoke to the original lineup of Living Colour that produced *Time's Up* and the ways in which they were successful because of the creative expression that comes out of Black Americans' unique experiences in the United States:

> Much was written about how we played the music, but it wouldn't have mattered what genre of music we explored and expressed ourselves with. There would have been a major impact because it was an extension of ourselves, of us. We all have Africa in common, meaning there is that feeling that only comes from people of African descent. Every culture has value. Every culture has a way

of expressing themselves, but there's something about the expression of people in America who have that African ancestry. What we do impacts everybody in major ways. And no other culture is any less valuable or any less special. So I would say it wouldn't have mattered what genre of music we would have decided to do. That chemistry that we had would have had impact.

These retrospective thoughts by Living Colour provide insight into what informed the second record and perhaps how that post-*Vivid* work might be perceived by the new fans. *Time's Up* was universally lauded by critics, and the members of Living Colour itself, and their production team, are proud of their efforts. As Reid states, "I think it's an extraordinary record. I mean, the sequence of it is really fascinating. And it's very much a journey in terms of what it's talking about, and the places it goes to." Will Calhoun also sees something special in their second album:

Time's Up was something that I walked away from satisfied in a different way than I did with *Vivid*. I was very happy with my first record. I knew it sounded amazing. I didn't give a shit about the success. I just knew what a great way to come on the scene. [With *Time's Up*] I felt so confident and proud of the effort. When I walked out of the studio that last day, I was so proud of what we accomplished. I was very proud of the whole project, maybe even a bit more than I was with *Vivid*. Something just felt different. I didn't feel that way the whole time afterwards. I had my moments when I said maybe, maybe I don't know.

Calhoun's doubt is referencing the commercial life of the album. It did very well in the United States immediately, but then sales tapered off. Was the record too experimental? Was it too Black for some fans? Glover has mixed feelings about the period right after *Time's Up* released. He has always been a shy person and a reluctant rock star, so he was not particularly excited to go on tour to support the album:

> If I'm going to spend the bulk of my time either in a hotel room or on a stage, I'd rather be home. Because I could stay in my own house. This is where all my stuff is. I got really sort of traumatized by the prospect of going back out on the road. I like making music. I like performing music—performing the music that I create, and the art that I create. It's people I have a problem with. And myself. That's who I have a problem with. It's not people. It's me.

As proud as he is of *Time's Up,* Glover, in retrospect, is also unsure if Living Colour should have followed up *Vivid* with an album that could prove more challenging to the casual fan:

> We were trying very hard to break away from *Vivid*, which was, in my estimation looking back at it, a mistake. We had time to break away. *Time's Up* is a brilliant record. But in terms of our career, that was a third or fourth record, not a second record. How do we keep going on a trajectory that we've been on? I think that our time in the limelight would have been much brighter and would last a little bit longer.

Glover certainly makes a compelling point. Would *Vivid II* have sold as well as *Vivid*? Could Living Colour have amassed so many fans that they would maintain a large core fanbase that would stick it out as they grew and evolved à la U2 or Bruce Springsteen had they kept the hits, or at least familiar and therefore popular songs, coming for a few more years? Or should artists always stay true to their evolving vision even if it may put their commercial career trajectory in jeopardy? Living Colour's choice to release an album as bold and compelling as *Time's Up* certainly did not go unnoticed with critics such as David Fricke noting "their deep-rooted spiritual resolve."[3]

Greg Tate saw it a little differently. For him, the band's Blackness made it necessary for Living Colour to push themselves harder than the average band might on their second album:

That record has an urgency that most people don't get with the sophomore record. Because they're Black and because we've made it there's *really* pressure. Black folks don't assume, "Oh, I got a top-40 record and a Grammy and shit. My life is set." It's like, "Yo, you better come with your *triple* A game this time . . . ." The fact that record starts with "Time's Up," which to me is also them kind of weaponizing their Bad Brains influence. "Oh we gonna make this *even* harder than anything the Brains has tried to do in one song." That to me is like where that energy of that record [comes from]. These boys just put whatever was on *Vivid*. . . . "Oh yeah, you know, we're putting this on like steroids and rocket fuel."

And after "Time's Up," the album would advance in unexpected directions. Tate continues:

> We're gonna move into some weird, loopy audio verité stuff about Africans and names and stuff. And then we're gonna do like an ultimate kind of anti-love, R&B ballad, and we're gonna do something else that sounds like South African Highlife music, and then we still got some bangers on here, so we got "Type" we gonna hit you with. . . . And then 'cause we want to let you know we're really like that Black band that got a attitude, we're gonna do a song called "Elvis Is Dead" with Public Enemy. Just to let you know, yeah, we're *those* Negroes too. . . . You know, so on one level, that record is made for everybody who both hated and loved the fact that a Black band was making it in the rock world of the 90s. They're right up there, in terms of profile with Nirvana, Jane's Addiction, Chili Peppers.

Doug Wimbish, who played his first show with the band at the 1992 Hollywood Rock Festival in São Paulo—Living Colour's last live commitment on the calendar before Skillings left—is also impressed by *Time's Up*.[4] When he met with the band to feel out playing together they were surprised when he chose to play "Time's Up" first. As Wimbish recounts, "I just chose the hardest song that they had at that time to play first. And that was 'Time's Up.'" "Time's Up" has proved to be one of Wimbish's favorite Living Colour songs:

> It's just fun because it's a release. And you have to really reenact that. It's not an R&B song. You're not playing the

Temptations at that time. It's kinda got some grit to it, but it also has attitude. It's like a microburst that's happening in the atmosphere that instead of the air going sideways, it's blowing down hard. . . . I love playing that song. I love watching the crowd as we're playing that song 'cause it just drives people into a frenzy. Or you have folks that aren't used to that be looking at you like you're crazy.

Time's Up offers a peek into the twenty-first century, an album that speaks to important social and political issues of that time, while also forecasting the most urgent concerns in the United States in the 2020s. Some of the album's considerations are problems that are historical and persist decade after decade, like police brutality, or the worsening situation we have with the environment, but also there was real prescience in a song like "Information Overload," which predicted the chaos of the internet. As Reid states:

It's a little unsettling. It's not so much that I buff my nails on my lapels and go hahaha. It really is a bit unsettling, and part of that is because it's not just about Akai sampling. It's like, history feels like a loop. And we've had these moments, not just of oppression, but we've had these moments of real progress.

Skillings puts it this way about the prophetic nature of many of *Time's Up's* lyrics:

I kind of call it the "accidental psychics." Some undesirable social conditions change for the better more rapidly than others. . . . I do not believe we were psychic or ahead of our time, so much as we were writing about social conditions, which were slow moving in terms of their improvement. And the movement in the direction of improvement has not been linear.

Time's Up is as strong of an album as anything Van Halen, Led Zeppelin, or the Red Hot Chili Peppers—bands critics have compared Living Colour to—has ever made. Living Colour has won consecutive Grammys, moved a lot of units, and created groundbreaking and timeless music. *And* they accomplished all that in an industry that was indifferent to rock artists who look like them until someone decided there was money to be made. Without Living Colour, there would be no Tom Morello and no Rage Against the Machine. As Morello offers:

> If you were a black guitar player, you probably loved Hendrix—which I did—but I couldn't admit it, I wanted to play Randy Rhoads! Living Colour changed that forever and they don't get credit for it. They came along right before Nirvana, Pearl Jam, Soundgarden and Jane's Addiction changed the ethos of rock and roll. I believe Living Colour deserves to be in that number because they changed the face of rock and roll. After Living Colour, that stigma was gone. It paved the way for a group like Rage Against the Machine, or a group like Soundgarden— bands that had people of colour in their midst. Until then, there was a real apartheid-like segregation on rock and roll radio.[5]

After Living Colour emerged the floodgates should have opened, but they didn't. That doesn't mean that Living Colour has not made a great impact or has not taught us much. Nor does this diminish their influence.

Then and now.

*   *   *

I watched the rest of Living Colour's set on that cold night in December 1990 from somewhere deep in the heart of the sweaty crowd. As I moved my body to the music—singing along, banging my head, screaming all wild with excitement—I knew that my worldview was changing, but I had no idea just how much it would be altered in the years to come. Living Colour (and Greg Tate, too) played no small role in my becoming a rock critic and journalist in my early thirties. And eventually, I learned more about my history as a doctoral student at UCLA through studying African American literature, history, and culture, with a focus on popular music in the United States, which is, of course, eternally indebted to the significant contributions of Black Americans. And now, I teach and write about African American literature and American popular music as a professor, scholar, and music journalist. How many other Black people, of all ages, saw (and see) themselves in Living Colour's music, and started bands or committed to other forms of creative and intellectual expression, infused with a love for Black people, and a knowledge of Black history, as a result?

I'm not the only one.

Acknowledgments

I started working on *Time's Up* in 2014 during the last year of my doctoral program in English at UCLA. I interviewed Vernon Reid and Corey Glover, capturing their words for a proposal I submitted to a 33 1/3 book series open call. My proposal was rejected, and I was disappointed, but when I put the proposal aside, I told myself that one day I would revise it and try again. That day came in summer 2020, and thankfully Corey, Vernon, and the rest of Living Colour were willing to talk, and they were interested in my telling the story of *Time's Up*. Untold hours of interviews, research, music listening, and writing made this book possible, and the entire process was truly a labor of love.

First and foremost, I want to thank all the members of Living Colour, present and past, who took time out of their busy schedules to speak with me, sometimes more than once, and after reading an early draft, offered helpful feedback and crucial fact-checking. Thank you to Will Calhoun, Corey Glover, Vernon Reid, Muzz Skillings, and Doug Wimbish. Thank you also to Dennis Diamond, Greg Drew, Paul Hamingson, and Ed Stasium for giving so generously of their time and for sharing vital and compelling information about the production of *Time's Up*. I am particularly indebted to Paul Hamingson for sharing the photos he took during the *Time's Up* recording sessions for reproduction in this book. Funding for the licensing fees was made possible by a University of Toledo URFO Small Award through the Office of Research and Sponsored Programs. It was also helpful to have had the opportunity to conduct one of several interviews for *Time's Up* with Vernon at the 2022 Pop Conference.

Thank you to Laina Dawes and Jill Rothenberg, who read drafts and offered helpful feedback. And a big thank you to Sean Maloney, my content editor for Bloomsbury, who, it turns out, was one of the readers of my accepted proposal back in 2020. I am grateful for his belief in this project, his incisive feedback, and his good cheer. I greatly appreciate Leah Babb-Rosenfeld's support for this project in its earliest stages and her and Rachel Moore's generous help throughout this process. I am also indebted to my friends in Los Angeles, New York, New Jersey, and Toledo, who offered much-needed support and crucial breaks to come up for air, especially during crunch time in summer 2022. And a special thank you to my dear friend Nzingha Clarke, who put me in touch with Corey and helped me reconnect with Vernon back in 2014.

Thank you also to my wonderful in-laws, Ann, Norm, Hillary, Alex, Lola, Liv, Peaches, and Perry for your unwavering love and affection. Thank you to my late mother, Jennifer, who inspired my passion for rock and roll and was there with me on the couch watching *It's Showtime at the Apollo* as I marveled at those four young Black men from NYC doing their *thing*. And thank you to my husband, Adam, who, as always, provided all manner of support for me and my work, including reading and offering helpful critiques on my book manuscript. And an extra special shout-out to sweet little Aloni, who has made my life better in every way possible.

Finally, thank you to the late Greg Tate, who talked to me for this book. Greg was my first writing mentor, who read my earliest and most embarrassing music criticism. This book is humbly dedicated to him.

Notes

Introduction

1   Mark Prado, *Living Colour: Beyond the Cult of Personality* (2020), 147–48.

2   "Artist: Living Colour," *Grammy Awards,* https://www.grammy.com/artists/living-colour/10625.

3   "Chart History: Living Colour," *Billboard*, https://www.billboard.com/artist/living-colour/chart-history/hsi/.

4   Armond White, *The Resistance: Ten Years of Pop Culture That Shook the World* (Woodstock: The Overlook Press, 1995), 87, 89.

5   Maureen Mahon, *Right to Rock: The Black Rock Coalition and the Cultural Politics of Race* (Durham and London: Duke University Press, 2004), 155.

6   Theodore Gracyk, *Rhythm and Noise: An Aesthetics of Rock* (Durham and London: Duke University Press, 1996), 180–1.

7   Mahon, *Right to Rock*, 159.

Chapter 1

1   Trey Ellis, "The New Black Aesthetic," *Callaloo* 38 (Winter, 1989): 233–43.

2   According to Mark Anthony Neal, *Soul Babies: Black Popular Culture and the Post-Soul Aesthetic* (New York: Routledge, 2002), 103, the post-soul ethos posits that "the generations(s) of black youth born after the early successes of the traditional civil rights movement are in fact divorced from the nostalgia associated with those successes and thus positioned to critically engage the movement's legacy from a state of objectivity that the traditional civil rights leadership is both unwilling and incapable of doing." For further discussion, please see Nelson George, *Buppies, B-boys, Baps, and Bohos: Notes on Post-Soul Black Culture* (Cambridge, MA: Da Capo Press, 2001) and Greg Tate, *Flyboy in the Buttermilk: Essays on Contemporary America* (New York: Simon and Schuster, 1992).

3   Notting Hill Riots (2005), [TV Program] BBC. https://www.youtube.com/watch?v=iaRCE7UUW0g

4   There are conflicting ideas about when the Notting Hill Riots began. Some sources suggest the Riots began on August 30, 1958, while acknowledging that there had been a ramping up of racial tensions for weeks prior. Other sources see an incident on August 23, 1958, where nine White men roved the streets looking for Black people to physically assault as the starting point for the riots. See Edward Pilkington, *Beyond the Mother Country: West Indians and the Notting Hill White Riots* (New York and London: Bloomsbury Academic, 2021) and Kathleen Paul, *Whitewashing Britain: Race and Citizenship in the Postwar Era* (Ithaca, NY: Cornell University Press, 1997).

5   BBC, "Notting Hill Riots."

6   Ibid.

7   Mark Olden, "White Riot: The Week Notting Hill Exploded,"
    The Independent, August 29, 2008, https://www.independent
    .co.uk/news/uk/home-news/white-riot-the-week-notting-hill
    -exploded-912105.html

Chapter 3

1   Walter Everett, "Pitch Down the Middle," in *Expression in Pop-
    Rock Music: Critical and Analytical Essays*, ed. Walter Everett
    (New York and London: Routledge, 2008), 111–74.

Chapter 4

1   David Fricke, "Living Colour's Time Is Now," *Rolling Stone*,
    November 1, 1990, https://www.rollingstone.com/music/
    music-news/living-colours-time-is-now-192320/.

2   Greg Kot, "Living Colour's Fury Fuels Band with Few Peers,"
    Chicago Tribune, November 8, 1990.

3   Fricke, "Living Colour's."

4   Prado, *Living Colour*, 112, 129, 199.

5   "Artist: Living Colour," *Grammy Awards*, https://www.
    grammy.com/artists/living-colour/10625.

6   Andy Aledort, "Message To Love – A Brief History of
    the Band of Gypsys," December 21, 2021, https://www
    .jimihendrix.com/editorial/message-to-love-a-brief-history-of
    -the-band-of-gypsys/.

7   Tom Turco, "Band Covers Spectrum," *The Shreveport Times*, March 17, 1989, 45, https://www.newspapers.com/image /217109150.

8   Ian Gittins, "Living Colour, Cindy Lee Berryhill: The Marquee, London," *Melody Maker*, July 16, 1988, http://www .rocksbackpages.com/Library/Article/living-colour-cindy-lee -berryhill-the-marquee-london.

9   Paul Lester, "Living Colour: Colour Shifts," *Melody Maker*, March 25,1989, http://www.rocksbackpages.com/Library/ Article/living-colour-colour-shifts.

10 George Varga, "Living Colour Says Elvis Is Dead, Racism Thrives," *The Daily Spectrum*, April 20, 1991, 13, https://www .newspapers.com/image/285453463.

11 Mahon, *Right to Rock*, 174, 268, 270.

12 Greg Prato, "Punk, Purity, and Positive Mental Attitude: The Turbulent Tale of Bad Brains," *Classic Rock*, June 9, 2020, https://www.loudersound.com/features/punk-purity-and -positive-mental-attitude-the-turbulent-tale-of-bad-brains.

13 "24-7 SPYZ: Early Albums to be Reissued," *BLABBERMOUTH.NET*, July 19, 2006, https://blabbermouth .net/news/spyz-early-albums-to-be-reissued.

14 Jacob Uitti, "Fishbone's Chris Dowd Talks the Band's Legendary History," *American Songwriter*, https:// americansongwriter.com/fishbones-chris-dowd-talks-the -bands-legendary-history/

15 Fricke, "Living Colour's."

16 Steve Hochman, "Colourizing the Rock Landscape: More than Prince or Michael Jackson, Living Colour has Reintroduced Rock to Its Black Music Heritage," *Los Angeles Times*, September 23, 1990.

17   Mark Lepage, "Stay Tuned as Living Colour Switches Channels of 90s Consciousness," *The Montreal Gazette*, September 8, 1990, 74, https://www.newspapers.com/image/423836338 (accessed January 14, 2022).

18   Scott Sutherland, "Living Colour Takes Place at Top of Rock," *The Burlington Free Press*, April 18, 1991, 36, https://www.newspapers.com/image/203170291.

19   Jon Pareles, New York Times News Service, "Righteous Rock," *The Palm Beach Post*, September 2, 1990, 280, https://www.newspapers.com/image/132423784.

20   L. Kent Wolgamott, "Hard Rock Reborn with Living Colour," *Lincoln Journal Star*, September 4, 1990, 13, https://www.newspapers.com/image/312458423.

21   Charles Shaar Murray, "Living Colour: *Time's Up*," *Q*, October 1990, http://www.rocksbackpages.com/Library/Article/living-colour-times-up.

22   Prado, *Living Colour*, 176–89.

23   John Leland, "Living Colour, Out of the Groove," *Newsday*, December 13, 1990, 111, https://www.newspapers.com/image/705935097

24   Peter Watrous, "Review/Music; Saxophonist and Living Colour," *New York Times,* December 16, 1990, https://www.nytimes.com/1990/12/16/arts/review-music-saxophonist-and-living-colour.html.

25   Prado, *Living Colour*, 188.

26   Michael Saunders, "Living Colour Takes Dead Aim at Rock," *New York Daily News*, December 13, 1990.

27   Kot, "Living Colour`s Fury."

Chapter 5

1 Prado, *Living Colour*, 157, 199.

2 "Artist: Living Colour," *Grammy Awards*, https://www.grammy.com/artists/living-colour/10625.

3 Fricke, "Living Colour's."

4 Prado, *Living Colour*, 239.

5 Tyler Damara Kelly, "Nine Songs: Tom Morello," *The Line of Best Fit*, December 3, 2021, https://www.thelineofbestfit.com/features/interviews/tom-morello-nine-favourite-songs.

Bibliography

"24-7 SPYZ: Early Albums to be Reissued."
    BLABBERMOUTH.NET, July 19, 2006. https://blabbermouth
    .net/news/spyz-early-albums-to-be-reissued.
Aledort, Andy. "Message To Love – A Brief History of the Band
    Of Gypsys." December 21, 2021. https://www.jimihendrix.com
    /editorial/message-to-love-a-brief-history-of-the-band-of
    -gypsys/.
"Artist: Living Colour." *Grammy Awards*. https://www.grammy.
    com/artists/living-colour/10625.
"Chart History: Living Colour." *Billboard*. https://www.billboard.
    com/artist/living-colour/chart-history/hsi/.
Ellis, Trey. "The New Black Aesthetic." *Callaloo* 38 (1989): 233–43.
Everett, Walter. "Pitch Down the Middle." In *Expression in Pop-
    Rock Music: Critical and Analytical Essays*, edited by Walter
    Everett, 111–74. New York and London: Routledge, 2008.
Fricke, David. "Living Colour's Time Is Now." *Rolling Stone*,
    November 1, 1990. https://www.rollingstone.com/music/music
    -news/living-colours-time-is-now-192320/.
George, Nelson. *Buppies, B-Boys, Baps & Bohos: Notes on Post-Soul
    Black Culture*. New York: Da Capo Press, 2001.
Gittins, Ian. "Living Colour, Cindy Lee Berryhill: The Marquee,
    London." *Melody Maker*, July 16, 1988. http://www

.rocksbackpages.com/Library/Article/living-colour-cindy-lee
-berryhill-the-marquee-london.

Gracyk, Theodore. *Rhythm and Noise: An Aesthetics of Rock*. Durham and London: Duke University Press, 1996.

Hochman, Steve. "Colourizing the Rock Landscape: More than Prince or Michael Jackson, Living Colour has Reintroduced Rock to Its Black Music Heritage." *Los Angeles Times*, September 23, 1990.

Humphreys, Dafydd. "Notting Hill Riots (BBC 2005)." YouTube video, 48:17. February 19, 2017. https://www.youtube.com/watch?v=iaRCE7UUW0g

Kelly, Tyler Damara. "Nine Songs: Tom Morello." *The Line of Best Fit*, December 3, 2021. https://www.thelineofbestfit.com/features/interviews/tom-morello-nine-favourite-songs

Kot, Greg. "Living Colour`s Fury Fuels Band with Few Peers." *Chicago Tribune*, November 8, 1990.

Leland, John. "Living Colour, Out of the Groove." *Newsday*, December 13, 1990, 111. https://www.newspapers.com/image/705935097

Lepage, Mark. "Stay Tuned as Living Colour Switches Channels of 90s Consciousness." *The Montreal Gazette*, September 8, 1990, 74. https://www.newspapers.com/image/423836338 (accessed January 14, 2022).

Lester, Paul. "Living Colour: Colour Shifts." *Melody Maker*, March 25, 1989. http://www.rocksbackpages.com/Library/Article/living-colour-colour-shifts.

Mahon, Maureen. *Right to Rock: The Black Rock Coalition and the Cultural Politics of Race*. Durham and London: Duke University Press, 2004.

Murray, Charles Shaar. "Living Colour: *Time's Up*." *Q*, October 1990. http://www.rocksbackpages.com/Library/Article/living-colour-times-up.

Neal, Mark Anthony. *Soul Babies: Black Popular Culture and the Post-Soul Aesthetic*. London: Routledge, 2002.

Olden, Mark. "White Riot: The Week Notting Hill Exploded." *The Independent*, August 29, 2008. https://www.independent.co.uk/news/uk/home-news/white-riot-the-week-notting-hill-exploded-912105.html

Pareles, Jon. New York Times News Service. "Righteous Rock." *The Palm Beach Post*, September 2, 1990, 280. https://www.newspapers.com/image/132423784.

Paul, Kathleen. *Whitewashing Britain: Race and Citizenship in the Postwar Era*. Ithaca, NY: Cornell University Press, 1997.

Pilkington, Edward. *Beyond the Mother Country: West Indians and the Notting Hill White Riots*. New York and London: Bloomsbury Academic, 2021.

Prado, Mark. *Living Colour: Beyond The Cult of Personality*. 2020.

Prato, Greg. "Punk, Purity, and Positive Mental Attitude: The Turbulent Tale of Bad Brains." *Classic Rock*, June 9, 2020. https://www.loudersound.com/features/punk-purity-and-positive-mental-attitude-the-turbulent-tale-of-bad-brains.

Saunders, Michael. "Living Colour Takes Dead Aim at Rock." *New York Daily News*, December 13, 1990.

Sutherland, Scott. "Living Colour Takes Place at Top of Rock." *The Burlington Free* Press, April 18, 1991, 36. https://www.newspapers.com/image/203170291.

Tate, Greg. *Flyboy in the Buttermilk: Essays on Contemporary America*. New York: Simon & Schuster, 1992.

Turco, Tom. "Band Covers Spectrum." *The Shreveport Times*, March 17, 1989, 45. https://www.newspapers.com/image/217109150 Downloaded.

Uitti, Jacob. "Fishbone's Chris Dowd Talks the Band's Legendary History." *American Songwriter*. https://americansongwriter.com/fishbones-chris-dowd-talks-the-bands- legendary-history/

Varga, George. "Living Colour Says Elvis Is Dead, Racism Thrives." *The Daily Spectrum*, April 20, 1991, 13. https://www.newspapers.com/image/285453463.

Watrous, Peter. "Review/Music; Saxophonist And Living Colour."
    New York Times, December 16, 1990. https://www.nytimes.com
    /1990/12/16/arts/review-music-saxophonist-and-living-colour
    .html.

White, Armond. *The Resistance: Ten Years of Pop Culture That
    Shook the World*. Woodstock: The Overlook Press, 1995.

Wolgamott, L. Kent. "Hard Rock Reborn with Living Colour."
    Lincoln Journal Star, September 4, 1990, 13. https://www
    .newspapers.com/image/312458423.

Also available in the series